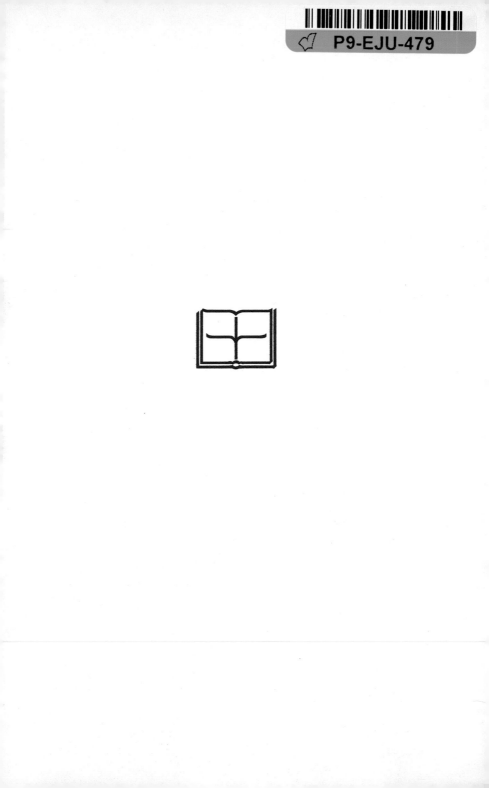

NEW TESTAMENT MESSAGE

A Biblical-Theological Commentary

Wilfrid Harrington, O.P. and Donald Senior, C.P.

EDITORS

New Testament Message, Volume 20

1 & 2 PETER

Donald Senior, C.P.

Michael Glazier, Inc.
Wilmington, Delaware

MICHAEL GLAZIER, INC.
1210A King Street
Wilmington, Delaware 19801

© 1980 by Michael Glazier, Inc.
All rights reserved.

Library of Congress Catalog Card Number: 80-65619
International Standard Book Number
New Testament Message series: 0-89453-123-9
1 & 2 PETER: 0-89453-143-3

Printed in the United States of America by Abbey Press

CONTENTS

Part III.
The Day of the Lord
2 Peter 3:1-18

EDITORS' PREFACE

New Testament Message is a commentary series designed
to bring the best of biblical scholarship to a wide audience.
Anyone who is sensitive to the mood of the church today is
aware of a deep craving for the Word of God. This interest
in reading and praying the scriptures is not confined to a
religious elite. The desire to strengthen one's faith and to
mature in prayer has brought Christians of all types and all
ages to discover the beauty of the biblical message. Our age
has also been heir to an avalanche of biblical scholarship.
Recent archaeological finds, new manuscript evidence, and
the increasing volume of specialized studies on the Bible
have made possible a much more profound penetration of
the biblical message. But the flood of information and its
technical nature keeps much of this scholarship out of the
hands of the Christian who is eager to learn but is not a
specialist. *New Testament Message* is a response to this
need.

The subtitle of the series is significant: "A Biblical-
Theological Commentary." Each volume in the series, while
drawing on up-to-date scholarship, concentrates on bringing to the fore in understandable terms the specific message of each biblical author. The essay-format (rather than
a word-by-word commentary) helps the reader savor the
beauty and power of the biblical message and, at the same
time, understand the sensitive task of responsible biblical
interpretation.

A distinctive feature of the series is the amount of space
given to the "neglected" New Testament writings, such as
Colossians, James, Jude, the Pastoral Letters, the Letters

of Peter and John. These briefer biblical books make a significant but often overlooked contribution to the richness of the New Testament. By assigning larger than normal coverage to these books, the series hopes to give these parts of Scripture the attention they deserve.

Because *New Testament Message* is aimed at the entire English speaking world, it is a collaborative effort of international proportions. The twenty-two contributors represent biblical scholarship in North America, Britain, Ireland and Australia. Each of the contributors is a recognized expert in his or her field, has published widely, and has been chosen because of a proven ability to communicate at a popular level. And, while all of the contributors are Roman Catholic, their work is addressed to the Christian community as a whole. The New Testament is the patrimony of all Christians.It is the hope of all concerned with this series that it will bring a fuller appreciation of God's saving Word to his people.

Wilfrid Harrington, O.P.
Donald Senior, C.P.

INTRODUCTION
TO THE PETRINE LETTERS

READING THE LETTERS of Peter can be like drawing some old family correspondence from the back of a desk drawer. We had seen the envelopes lying there now and then but had never taken the time to pull them out. Then in a moment of leisure we do read them and our memory swells with names and incidents almost forgotten. We are reminded, too, that with all the rush of time some things seem never to change: the same persons, the same hopes and pains. And we might also discover that old letters sometimes seem to hold fresh wisdom.

The letters of Peter surely have been back drawer in the New Testament and in the life of the church. The First Letter of Peter has fared much better than the Second but neither could be considered a "popular" biblical book. It would be a shame for this christian correspondence to yellow in the envelopes for too long. Both letters, but especially 1 Peter, are filled with provocative insights into the christian life. Even though we are separated from the original writers and readers by time, culture, and geography, they are family letters and this generation can learn from them. The questions that swirl through the church today have some tantalizing parallels in the subjects of these ancient texts: responsibility to secular culture, lay spirituality, minority status in an unchristian society, respect for creation, feminism, the mystery of suffering, uncertainty about the future. All of these human and christian problems are taken up in earnest by these two letters. To read them in a spirit of prayer and reflection is not an idle task for a moment of leisure, but something worth our serious effort.

The two letters both bear the name of Peter but they are vastly different. Their literary styles sharply contrast: 1 Peter is warm, vibrant, richly biblical in its imagery; 2 Peter is stiff, violently polemical, steeped in abstract Greek terminology. They were surely written by two different authors at different periods of early history. Although no precise dating is possible (cf. the discussion that follows), it seems clear that 1 Peter wrote sometime in the 70's or 80's while 2 Peter wrote after the turn of the century, perhaps the last of the New Testament books. The two letters may have been sent to the same general area in Asia Minor, but circumstances had changed so much in the intervening decades that there was no common audience for the two works.

Two Letters "From Peter"

There are, however, common bonds between the two letters in addition to their recognized position as inspired and canonical writings of the New Testament. First of all, both letters claim *Petrine authorship* (cf. 1 Pt 1:1; 2 Pt 1:1). It is unlikely that Peter himself actually penned either of the letters. This does not make the claims of the letters deceptive. Under certain circumstances, it was acceptable for ancient writers to use a literary device called pseudonymity whereby an author, invoking the name of a famous and now departed hero or leader, could write a letter of instruction in his name. Several New Testament letters (e.g., the Pastoral letters and probably some later Pauline material such as Ephesians) use this device. This literary form is most clearly at work in 2 Peter. The rather elaborate Greek style of the letter, its constant use of hellenistic terminology and religious concepts, its concern with such pastoral questions as the denial of the second coming and misinterpretation of Paul's letters are evidence that this letter could not have been written by Peter the Palestinean Jew who died around 64 A.D. Yet the author goes further than 1 Peter to stress that Peter is the writer; using the Hebrew form of his name (1:1), referring to his impending death (1:14), recalling his eyewitness presence at the transfiguration (1:16-19), alluding to his "first letter" (3:1) and to his association with Paul (3:15). Paradoxically, the chronological distance of the author from the time of Peter means that he must give more elaboration to the literary device of pseudonymity.

1 Peter, on the other hand, is more subtle. Peter's name is invoked at the beginning of the letter (1:1), but in only one other place (5:1) is his apostolic role alluded to and then in very general terms as "a fellow elder and a witness of the sufferings of Christ." There are significant references to "Silvanus, a faithful brother" (5:12) and "my son Mark" (5:13), both prominent members of the early church (cf. below). The lighter hand of 1 Peter may be due to the fact that this letter is much closer to the historical era of Peter the apostle. The rather polished Greek style of the letter, the degree of organization apparently already achieved in the church (e.g., elders are appointed or elected and salaried— cf. chapter 5), and the letter's contact with developed Pauline theology are facts that argue strongly, but not decisively, against authentic Petrine authorship. Indeed the lack of a clear-cut case has led many New Testament scholars, including some very recent ones, to affirm Peter as the author.

However, the well-developed theology of the letter and some internal leads suggest a "compromise" solution. It seems certain that Peter the apostle did come to Rome for a period of time before his death in the mid 60's. This city is the "Babylon" referred to in 1 Peter (cf. 5:13). The letter also mentions two significant members of the early church: Silvanus (5:12) and Mark (5:13). Both of these were associated with Peter *and* Paul in the early mission of the church. Silvanus, also known in the New Testament by the Aramaic form of his name Silus, comes on the scene in Acts at the Council of Jerusalem. He, along with Judas Barsabbas, is an elder of the Jerusalem church selected to accompany Paul and Barnabas to Antioch in order to promulgate the decree of the council (cf. Acts 15:22-35). After Barnabas and Paul have a falling out, Silvanus (Silus) accompanies Paul on his second missionary journey (cf. Acts 16-18). Paul himself refers to his missionary work with Silvanus in 2 Corinthians 1:19, 1 Thessalonians 1:1 and 2 Thessalonians 1:1. Mark or John Mark as he is called in some texts (cf. Acts 12:12) also had key associations with Peter and Paul. Peter stayed at John Mark's house after his escape from prison (Acts 12:12). And it seems that Mark was in Jerusalem during the time of the council (cf. Acts 13:13). Mark also had some intriguing contacts with Paul, accompanying him and Barnabas on their first missionary tour (cf. Acts 12:25) but apparently abandoning the mission (13:13) and thereby incurring Paul's disfavor (16:38). An altercation over Mark led to a breakup of the Paul and Barnabas team (16:39-40). The latter non-biblical tradition reported by Papias places Mark at Rome in the company of Peter.

The fact that all three—Peter, Silvanus and Mark—are mentioned in this letter from Rome may explain the letter's unique blend of ideas and its Petrine authorship. Silvanus— and to a lesser degree John Mark—would be familiar with Paul's thought. This would explain the fact that there are many Pauline ideas in 1 Peter but few, if any, direct quotations from Paul's writing. In other words, Silvanus brought with him a sound sense of Pauline tradition. All three would have been concerned with the universal sweep of th christian mission. If Luke's portrayal of Peter is to have any credibility, Peter ultimately became the champion of a gentile mission and mediator between the Jewish and gentile branches of the young church. Even Paul's rebuke to Peter for caving into Jewish-christian pressures by not eating with gentiles in Antioch (cf. Gal 2:11-14) is a left-handed acknowledgement of Peter's mediating role. Thus a small group of missionary leaders seems to have assembled at Rome in the early 60's. They were well aware of Paul's mission theology and had strong roots in Judaism and biblical tradition. They had extensive experience in the missionary efforts of the church, had traveled widely, and were concerned with the relationships among the local churches.

1 Peter is a letter whose ultimate source was this key apostolic group. It is probable that the letter was not written during Peter's lifetime (although this is not self-evident). It may have been written later by Silvanus. This could be the meaning of 5:12: "By Silvanus . . . I have written briefly to you." Although another interpretation could be that Silvanus is the secretary (as Tertius is for Paul in Rom 16:22) or the carrier of the letter to the churches in Asia Minor. Any of these are possible but I am inclined to think that neither Peter nor Silvanus are directly involved in the *literary* production of the letter. Both are mentioned (along with John Mark) to signal to the readers the origin of the traditions contained in the letter and the authority that backs it up. An author formed by this group would have written the letter at a later date perhaps in the 70's or 80's to encourage the far-flung churches of Asia Minor. He writes in the name of Peter because Peter is the most authoritative figure in the group. We do not know the attitude of the Christians in Asia Minor towards Peter. There is no evidence that he evangelized these areas. Some Jews from these regions are mentioned among the crowds who heard Peter's Pentecost discourse (Acts 2:9). From these and other christian missionaries, the communities must have known of Peter and his important role as one of the first followers of Jesus, as spokesman for the disciples, as witness to the resurrection, and as leader in the church's early mission. In any case, the author of 1 Peter feels free to write in Peter's name and can presume the authority of his words without any elaborate explanation. For the recipients it must have made sense that "Peter" had the right not only to encourage individual Christians but to advise their "elders" (cf. chapter 5:1).

The hypotheses of such a Petrine group at Rome brings us back to the bond between the two Petrine letters. 2 Peter is written much later than 1 Peter, probably as late as the first quarter of the second century. But it, too, invokes Peter's name and authority and even explicitly refers to the first letter (3:1). It seems probable that this letter, too, originates from Rome and was directed to the same general region as 1 Peter. It is concerned with "unity" questions but now more on the level of sound teaching and orthodoxy. The threat to the churches is not simply their minority status in the pagan world but the internal threat of false teachers and wrong interpretation of the tradition. These later concerns sharply differentiate the two letters, but, at the same time, link them on the level of pastoral strategy. The writer of the letter obviously believes that the name and authority of "Peter" would have some impact on the errant community. This is the same kind of assumption that 1 Clement can make in writing from Rome to Corinth at about the same stage of the church's development (early second century).

These two letters, then, point to an emerging Petrine tradition and a ministry of unity in the church some time after the death of the historical Peter. It would be rash to conclude on the basis of these two letters alone to a highly organized central authority in the early church. Yet the existence of the two letters from Peter—whether actually written in his lifetime (possible only in the case of 1 Peter) or pseudonymous—is a significant fact for early church history and a focus of growing ecumenical reflection (on this point confer the inter-denominational study, *Peter in the New Testament*).

Where Are We Going—A Christian View of the Future

There is another important link between 1 and 2 Peter that should be noted. Both letters are convinced that having a strong sense of the *future* is essential to being a good Christian. By future both authors mean not the impossible-to-discern events of tomorrow or the next decade, but the *ultimate* future, the final movement of all of world history to God. Each author is convinced that humanity is part of an ongoing story. Creation and human history are not a monotonous treadmill or a swirl of chaos. Everything—even suffering and death—mysteriously fits into the destiny shaped by a compassionate God. All the world inches forward, even if imperceivable to us, toward a rendezvous with the Lord.

The first letter of Peter dwells on the glorious and hope-filled aspects of history's climax. It promises an "imperishable inheritance," a moment of "glory" when all the world will break out in praise of its God (1:3-5; 2:12). The author is convinced that the remaining chapters of the human story are brief: the end will be "soon" (1:6; 4:7, 17). The second letter, by contrast, dwells on the dark side of the endtime. Because the promised transformation of the world necessarily means that conditions we now know are transitory, he speaks of the destruction and purification of the world by fire. The end will come as judgement upon those who waste their lives and live in falsehood. But for 2 Peter, too, that destruction is not final but merely prelude to a "new heavens and a new earth" (3:13), the fulfillment of God's "precious and very great promises" (1:4). For 2 Peter the endtime is not near; as humans reckon time it is still distant, distant enough to lead some to abandon any hope in it (3:3-4).

Neither author dwells on this final future as a means of escape from present responsibilities. Theirs is not a "pie-in-the-sky" christianity. For 1 Peter the promise of a world shot through with glory is an incentive to hope *now* and a call for full involvement in the structures of human society. The Christian must give a "testimony of hope" to a weary world (3:15) and work even with hostile groups in society to nudge the world forward towards the goal of God's creation. For 2 Peter, by contrast, the promised transformation of the world serves as a sober warning to Christians who have severely weakened their commitment to the gospel and who cave into the false allurements of the world. Faithful Christians should reflect on the future in order to find the strength to be stable as they work out their salvation now in history (3:9-13).

The convictions of both authors about the destiny of the world are ultimately optimistic and stem from the heart of biblical tradition. Israel always trusted in God's promises. So did Jesus, whose parables are filled with images of hope— Kingdoms coming, seeds bearing the promise of growth, a Father waiting at the end of the road. The death and resurrection of Jesus became both the pattern and the guarantee of what all of creation can expect. The authors of these early christian letters were convinced that to lose this part of the tradition would be to lose the gospel itself. This may be the most challenging message that the letters offer to the contemporary church. Do we believe in the future? Are we convinced that all of human history moves toward God—or, perhaps better put—that God is moving towards us? Does the christian vision of a world destined for glory, for transformation, have anything to say about our social responsibility and our mission in an era of history beginning to choke with self-doubt?

These old family letters might have something explosive to say to a modern church.

Acknowledgements

As my work on this commentary comes to a close, I would like to thank some of those who helped me: Sr. Kay Sheskaitis, I.H.M. who patiently typed the manuscript and whose quick eye rescued me from more than one mistake; Wilfrid Harrington, O.P. for his friendship and encouragement all during our collaboration on the *New Testament Message* series; and in the spirit of 1 Peter, I want to express a special word of thanks to the many sterling lay men and women who have taught me the meaning of the gospel and given me reason to hope, beginning with my own family and stretching to such people as Michael and Joan Glazier, whose ministry of the word is a labor of love.

Commentary
on 1 Peter

AN INTRODUCTION
TO 1 PETER

1 PETER MAY BE the New Testament's most exuberant book. The letter pulsates with joy, with surging hope, with optimism. Yet, paradoxically, it dwells on the question of suffering—that of Jesus and that of the Christian—with unparalleled single-mindedness. Before opening the pages of this great christian letter a few additional words of introduction may be in order.

The Occasion of the Letter

The Christians of northern Asia Minor to whom this letter from Rome was directed are called "exiles" (1:1) and "aliens" (2:11). This is an important hint as to the occasion which prompted the letter. These scattered christian communities were lonely outposts in a hostile world. Their "exile" status was not caused by some political ban or by deportation from one region to another. They were native to the region, Jewish and gentile converts from the culturally mixed population of Asia Minor. Theirs was an exile of the spirit, the exile that results from being out of step with the values and goals of the predominant society surrounding them. These Christians had chosen a different way of life. That difference made them suspect in the eyes of their non-christian neighbors (cf. 1 Pt 4:3-4). The suffering frequently referred to in 1 Peter resulted not from systematic state persecution (something that the church would suffer only decades later in this part of the Roman empire) but from the ridicule and oppression that a dominant culture can inflict on a minority in a host of cruel ways.

3

Even though scattered across a somewhat remote section of the Empire, these Christians were not abandoned. Their plight was of concern to a christian leader in Rome, a member of the Petrine group prominent in that church (cf. the general Introduction). He writes in the name of Peter to the local churches and their leaders, reminding them of their magnificent baptismal call and encouraging them to live in hope. He chooses a style of literature that was already becoming popular in christian circles. Letter writing was not, of course, a christian invention, but Paul had used the medium of letters to keep in touch with the communities he had evangelized or which he intended to visit. His letters were a blend of the personal and the public, enabling them to address problems of a specific community but universal enough to circulate to other groups of Christians as time went on. A large percentage of the New Testament books would adopt a letter or epistle format, even when the contents departed from the kind of message associated with letter writing (cf., for example, the Epistle of James or the Apocalypse). Peter's letter is explicitly directed to several churches (1:1), presuming that the message will be circulated from one to the next. This fact alone shows the strong sense of kinship that individual local churches felt with other christian communities.

The Unity of the Letter

Some scholars have questioned whether this New Testament book originated as a letter. The explicit reference to baptism in 3:21 and frequent allusions to the sacrament in the central part of the letter have led to the suggestion that the original core was a homily addressed to catechumens on the occasion of their baptism. A later editor would have added material and shaped the whole into its present letter format. Other scholars note the liturgical tone of certain parts of the letter (e.g., the prayers of praise and the response "Amen" in 4:11 and 5:10-11, snatches of hymns or creeds such as 2:21-24 or 3:18-22, the frequent use of quasi-liturgical terms such as "glory" or *paschein,* the Greek word for "suffering") and surmise that the author may have built his letter around portions of an ancient baptismal or Easter liturgy. Questions about the original unity of the letter are also raised because of the apparent difference in tone between the section ending with "amen" in 4:11 and that beginning in 4:12. In the previous part, 1 Peter seems to refer to suffering as a future threat, in the concluding section as a present reality.

But almost all of these alleged cracks in the letter's facade may be the result of scholars' spending too much time behind the microscope. When one goes through the letter from start to finish, as the commentary that follows will do, there is overwhelming evidence of its unity. The author does use fragments of hymns, scripture quotations and perhaps pieces of early creeds. But these are all blended into a coherent whole. There is no rigidly logical structure to the letter but there is an overall sense of movement and purpose. After a brief greeting (1:1-2), the author begins his first major section (1:3-2:10) which recalls the foundations of christian existence, a joyous recital of what it means to be a member of God's people. The second major section stretches from 2:11 to 4:11; here the author urges his Christians to live in a way that fits their call. Here is where the author spells out his strong convictions about discipleship in the world. A final section (4:12-5:14) closes the letter, summarizing the main themes and reminding the Christians of the inevitability of suffering. Throughout all of these sections the author maintains a coherent and consistent vision of christian life. This vision is the guarantee of the letter's literary and theological unity.

The Message of the Letter

As we noted above, 1 Peter is a startling blend of joy and suffering. Few biblical books can match its sense of cosmic optimism, its evident enthusiasm for life; yet the letter refers to the sufferings of Jesus more than any other New Testament book.

The concentration on the passion of Jesus is the key to the letter's message. The author lingers over Jesus' agonizing struggle from death to life because this is the decisive pattern of all christian existence, indeed of all human existence. Jesus the "just one" was put to death but the power of God brought him to life (3:18). This was not merely a personal drama for Jesus; it was his mission—that he should "die for sins," "the righteous for the unrighteous." Neither Jesus nor the Christians nor, for that matter, any human being could wink at the reality of suffering and death that crowds our world. But the message of the gospel, a message embodied in Jesus, was that life has the last word. Drawing on the deepest of New Testament traditions, the author of 1 Peter orchestrates this death-life theme to the full: it is the meaning of baptism, the basis for christian hope, the motivation and content of christian witness, and the final verdict on human destiny.

The goal of the letter, as suggested above, was to encourage christian "exiles" under the pressures of an aggressively secular culture. But it is important to note that the author hands out advice only after he has constructed a breathtaking vision of what christian life is all about. In the first major section (1:3–2:10) and in scattered passages throughout the letter, the author musters vivid biblical metaphors and invokes christian experience to remind his fellow Christians of their awesome beauty as God's chosen ones and as his living temple (cf. especially 2:4-10). Only then does the author discuss with them the hard tasks of faithful discipleship. This pattern—first the gospel, then the call for responsible living—is an approach to preaching too often forgotten. Here is an almost subliminal message of 1 Peter that the modern church should consider.

One of the major contributions of 1 Peter is the robust sense of christian mission he conveys. Even though these fragile communities are embedded in a hostile environment and suffering abuse, he does not prescribe reaction or caution. The Christians are not to flee the world but to participate in it (cf. 2:13). They are not to condemn or berate the world, but to treat it with respect, even gentleness, all with the hope that in its own time the world will join the Christians in glorifying God. There is no hint of a "ghetto" mentality in the entire letter: on the contrary, a case could be made that 1 Peter has a more positive attitude to secular society than any other New Testament writing.

Two basic principles undergird the christian vocation according to 1 Peter (cf. the discussion under 2:11-12). The first is a call to be an active participant in the structures of the world. The Christian is not to withdraw from the institutions of human society, even when they present conflicts with one's beliefs. Instead one must "submit," participate "for the Lord's sake," because in leading an authentic christian life in the midst of the world one can further the creative task of God himself as he moves the world to its destiny. The author singles out particularly difficult examples to drive home his point; christian slaves living under cruel masters, christian wives trying to be faithful to hostile and non-believing husbands. The second principle must accompany the first. To have the strength and determination to live in the world with integrity, the Christian must experience "inner freedom" (2:11, 16). Destructive "passions" and desires must be let go of. The Christian must keep his or her eye fixed on Jesus and nourish the experience of conversion. Nowhere in the letter does the author underestimate the cost of discipleship. Evil is a reality, an aggressive reality that prowls the world seeking to devour the naive and indulgent (5:8-9).

On the basis of what we will call a "witness spirituality," 1 Peter gives positive orientation to the churches. His advice is not directed merely to the individual Christian; his scope is also communal. The love and service that binds the Christians together as God's household are the most potent witness they can offer a world starved for meaning (1:22; 3:8-9; 4:8-11).

This forceful message is what makes 1 Peter an uncommon New Testament book. The twentieth century has been a time of revolution. Technological advance has quickened the pace of secularization at the same time that it has created hunger for religious meaning. A succession of horrors—two world wars, the Holocaust, the threat of nuclear extinction, to name a few—have put the future in doubt and created a vacuum of hope. At the same time the churches have experienced their own deep changes. This is particularly true for Roman Catholicism. In western churches, at least, the spirit of the Second Vatican Council and the emergence of educated and committed lay people have challenged styles of authority and descriptions of the christian vocation long dominated by a clerical mentality. All of these vital questions and many others could benefit from the powerful message of this letter. 1 Peter maintains a buoyant sense of hope in spite of suffering. It addresses its message to a church that is first of all the people of God united in baptism and exercising their discipleship in the midst of the world. It refuses to believe that even a very secular world is anything less than sacred. Mysteriously, providentially, this old letter is a letter for our time.

GREETING: FROM PETER TO THE EXILES. (1:1-2).

1 Peter, an apostle of Jesus Christ,
    To the exiles of the Dispersion in Pontus, Galatia, Cappadocia, Asia, and Bithynia, ²chosen and destined by God the Father and sanctified by the Spirit for obedience to Jesus Christ and for sprinkling with his blood:
    May grace and peace be multiplied to you.

Peter's letter begins as most letters do: with a greeting for the ones to whom it is sent. As in the letters of Paul, the author uses a conventional form of Greco-Roman letter writing ("from [author's name] to [addressee's name], greetings") but expands it with sentiments drawn from Christian life and prayer. The thoughts tucked into this opening line signal a number of themes that will break into full view later in the epistle.

The text begins with an unflinching assertion of the author's identity: "Peter an apostle of Jesus Christ." Many of Paul's epistles begin with a similar label, but the Apostle of the Gentiles usually appends some explanatory phrase defending the legitimacy of his claim (e.g., in Galatians, "Paul an apostle—not from men, but through Jesus Christ and God the Father...*"). But Peter's claim is unquestioned by the gospel tradition or by Paul (implicitly in Gal 1:18; 2:7; 1 Cor 15:5). He is recognized as one chosen by Jesus to be the leader in the community (cf. Mt 16:13-19) and is a central figure in the early church's mission. To him belongs the title "apostle," literally "one sent" by Jesus Christ.

As we have discussed in the Introduction, it is not certain that Peter himself is the actual author of this epistle. Nevertheless, the assertion of his name and title at the head of this letter written to a group of churches in Asia Minor (cf. below) is a significant witness to Petrine influence in the early church. At the conclusion of the letter (5:1) Peter's role will be reasserted; in the intervening material his name or personal authority are not invoked.

The addressees of the letter are also significant: "the exiles of the Dispersion in Pontus, Galatia, Cappadocia, Asia and Bithynia." These are regions in the northern part of Asia Minor, present day Turkey. Some suggest that the listing actually charts the route along which this circular letter would be carried. Paul had evangelized some of these areas but there is no evidence that Peter had been in this part of the world. That he or a letter written in his name would be addressed to these christian communities without apology or explanation testifies to the authority attached to the name of Peter at this early stage of the church.

The first words that draw us into the remarkable theology of 1 Peter are "exiles of the Dispersion." The Christians in these churches are not "exiles" in the technical sense of being forcibly displaced from their homeland. Theirs is a *spiritual* exile, people whose commitments and values place them at odds with the worldview of the society to which they belong (cf. 4:3-4). As the rest of the letter will illustrate, Peter does not encourage these "exiles" to indulge in self-pity or to barricade themselves from the hostility of the world around them. On the contrary this letter sees "exile" as an opportunity to preach the gospel and to transform the world. That upbeat note is subtly affirmed in the word "Dispersion" or diaspora, a term used by Judaism to refer to their people scattered throughout the Mediterranean world. These Jews were separated from their homeland but were still members of God's people and heirs to his promises. Now the scattered Christians, despite their exile, are God's people and their destiny is in his hands.

The optimistic mood of 1 Peter breaks out into the open in the second verse of the greeting. Using language that may have been part of an early baptismal liturgy (note the reference to Father, Son, Spirit), the author gives a condensed description of the origin and mission of christian existence. These "exiles" are "chosen" by God. This word has more significance for the author than our translation seems to indicate. In the actual wording of the Greek text, "chosen" is the first name Peter gives the Christians (literally, "to the chosen, exiles of the dispersion"). This sense of "election" was one of the deepest beliefs of the Jews in the Old Testament: in spite of their insignificance, simply because he loved them, God chose them to be his people (cf. the beautiful text of Dt 7:6-8). This was a rockbed foundation for the early Christians as well: God the Father had chosen them, given them new life, and offered them an incredible destiny as his people. The first major section of the letter (cf. 1:3-2:10) will dwell on this theme.

This christian call is worked out through the sanctifying power of the Spirit. The text literally says: "in the holiness of the Spirit." As we shall see, 1 Peter is very interested in "holiness," in the practical values and decisions that make a Christian's life a genuine manifestation of God. This work of holiness is further described as a call "to obedience." This does not mean a slavish carrying out of orders; rather it suggests that our lives must be in harmony with the truth (cf. 1:22 where the author speaks of "obedience to the truth"), the ultimate truth of being called by God to be his people. A final descriptive phrase might strike a modern reader as bizarre: "for sprinkling with the blood of Jesus Christ." The words draw on the Old Testament theology of covenant. Exodus 24:3-8 recounts the ceremony in which the people pledged their obedience to the Sinai covenant. The sprinkling of the people and the altar with blood (a sign of life itself for the Jews) symbolized the new life-bond between Yahweh and Israel. The author of our epistle uses this vivid image to describe the bond between the Christians and their God. The "blood" that seals the bond and becomes the basis for christian obedience to God's will is the person and mission of Jesus. As 1:18-20 will explicitly note, Christ's death and resurrection are the basis of our redemption as God's people.

The images heaped into this greeting—election, holiness, reference to the Trinity, covenant—all suggest that the author is reflecting on the meaning of baptism. At several points in the first half of the letter (explicitly in 3:21) a theology of baptism is evident. As noted in the Introduction to the commentary, some scholars have even suggested that the original form of the epistle was a baptismal instruction. Although the meaning of baptism is certainly a concern of the letter, it is not its prime purpose. Rather, the author concentrates on exhorting his readers to *live out* the call to holiness which their baptism signifies.

The greeting concludes with a succinct wish that "grace" and "peace" be multiplied to them. Neither term is an idle cliche for our author. As the rest of the letter will demonstrate, "grace" as God's gifts of life and support to the suffering Christian and "peace" as the effect of God's nourishing presence are life lines for those who are "in exile."

Part I.

Born to Hope—
The Foundations of Christian Experience
1:3-2:10.

The greeting concluded, the letter now moves to an exultant review of the origin and nature of christian life. This first major section which stretches into the middle of chapter 2 begins with a triumphant burst of praise for God's mercy, takes note of the sufferings that Christians experience, reviews the history of human longing for salvation and its fulfillment in Jesus, and concludes with a stirring description of the church. All of this serves as a basis for a series of directives and encouragements which the author begins in 2:11, the second major section of the epistle.

BLESSED BE GOD—WE ARE BORN TO A LIFE OF HOPE!
1:3-5.

> ³Blessed be the God and Father of our Lord Jesus Christ! By his great mercy we have been born anew to a living hope through the resurrection of Jesus Christ from the dead, ⁴and to an inheritance which is imperishable, undefiled, and unfading, kept in heaven for you, ⁵who by God's power are guarded through faith for a salvation ready to be revealed in the last time.

Most of Paul's letters follow up the initial greeting with an encouraging passage giving thanks to God for the faith and goodness of the christian community he addressed.

1 Peter has a similar opening section but it is less a personal prayer for the recipients than a triumphant acclamation of praise to God for the christian life that he and his fellow Christians share. The tone of this passage and much of the rest of 1 Peter can be described as "liturgical," shot through with a sense of praise and worship. One of the most enticing qualities of this epistle is the way the author blends a lilting mood of hope and optimism with an open-eyed awareness of suffering.

The root cause of such hope begins to be acknowledged in these verses. "The God and Father of our Lord Jesus Christ" (a thoroughly christian designation for the God of Israel) is praised because out of pure mercy and love we have been born to a new life of hope. The gift of christian life is described as a "rebirth;" through God's call and through baptism the Christian leaves behind a life of despair and meaninglessness (cf. 2:10; 4:3-4) and begins a new life filled with hope. The image of "being born again" (used here and in 1:23) is also found in John's Gospel (3:5, 7; cf. also 1:13), and in Titus 3:5 referring to the beginning of christian existence through baptism. The ultimate root of this metaphor may be the powerful biblical theme of redemption as a new creation (cf., for example, Is 65:17-25), although the image of "being born again" is not found in the Old Testament as such.

The author uses two sets of phrases to describe the destiny of this new life; it is birth "to living hope" and to an "imperishable inheritance." Hope is one of the deepest currents in the theology of 1 Peter. Living hope belongs to the Christian because of the resurrection of Jesus Christ from the dead. God's faithful mercy which brought Jesus from death to life is also exercised on behalf of the Christian—and that ultimate expression of God's mercy is the ground for our hope. The image of an inheritance "kept in heaven" expresses the same conviction although in more future-oriented terms. Confidence in a glorious heritage was a basic impulse for biblical hope beginning with the pilgrimage of Abraham, accelerated by the experience of exodus and undaunted through the pain of exile and defeat. Israel continued to trust that God would be faithful to his promises. That same conviction is expressed here. Hope in a future inheritance, however, is not without significance for the *present*. The promise of such a destiny should transform the way Christians look at their world *now*: this will be the point of much of the letter's exhortations (cf. the key text of 3:15).

A final description of the "reborn" Christian closes out the section. They are the ones who "by God's power are guarded . . . for salvation." The powerful saving God stands watch over his beloved people. Although the image is muscular, the phrase "through faith" emphasizes that this care is a result of the love and trust that unites a merciful God with his chosen people. The full breadth of the "salvation" we are promised will only be revealed "in the last time," that is, at the consummation of the world. Here again our epistle affirms one of the basic visions of the bible. The full experience of redemption will only come when all injustice, pain and death are swept away (cf. the great visions of Is 25:6-9; 65:17-25; Apoc 21:1-8).

JOY IN THE MIDST OF PAIN.
1:6-9.

> [6]In this you rejoice, though now for a little while you may have to suffer various trials, [7]so that the genuineness of your faith, more precious than gold which though perishable is tested by fire, may redound to praise and glory and honor at the revelation of Jesus Christ. [8]Without having seen him you love him; though you do not now see him you believe in him and rejoice with unutterable and exalted joy. [9]As the outcome of your faith you obtain the salvation of your souls.

As the address "exiles" has already hinted (1:1), the Christians to whom this letter is sent are suffering. This is a fact that the author cannot and does not ignore—no other New

Testament writing reflects on the meaning of suffering with the intensity of 1 Peter. In these verses the mood is still upbeat, carried over from the burst of praise begun in verse 3. The Christians "rejoice" (vv. 6, 9), but that joy must co-exist with the reality of suffering.

The meaning of the opening phrase is not completely clear. "In *this*" presumably refers to the immediately preceding word *kairos*, the final "age," although by extension the source of joy is the whole range of ideas expressed in the previous section: God's mercy, our rebirth to hope, our inheritance of salvation. The verb "rejoice" could be construed as an imperative: "rejoice in this"! But the indicative, as in our translation, is probably the correct meaning.

What is clear in this text is how the author chooses to interpret the meaning of suffering in this first explicit reference to it in the letter. Suffering, he asserts, can be experienced as a purification during the brief time before the end of the world. The notion of suffering as a "test" or "trial" was explored in the wisdom tradition of the Old Testament where the image of fire purging precious metal is applied to suffering as a purification of one's faith in God (cf. Wis 3:5-6). This conviction is not deducible from abstract principles but comes from experience. The sufferings that come to a believer because of his or her christian faith (the kind of suffering that 1 Peter seems to have in mind) can "test" the strength of one's faith and deepen it; this has been the experience of persecuted Christians from the first century to the present day. Even the seemingly arbitrary sufferings brought on by illness or accident—although they remain tragic and unglamorous—can purify the humanity and the faith of the one who endures them.

The letter goes beyond speaking of suffering as mere clenched-teeth endurance. The author affirms that even in the midst of suffering the Christian has a right to joy, one of the gifts the bible always associated with the experience of God's salvation. Not only does the suffering Christian rejoice but the trials he or she endures have themselves a salvific purpose: they "redound to praise and glory and honor" when Jesus is manifested at the end of the world. The belief that suffering borne in faith has the power to bring about the transformation of the world is a major theme developed in subsequent sections of the letter.

Up to this point the author has been reflecting on the great mercy of God the Father who calls us to salvation, even in the midst of suffering. But the reference to the consummation of the world as "the revelation of Jesus Christ" seems to turn the author's attention to the person of Jesus. In beautifully poetic words the text speaks of loving Jesus and believing in him even though this must be faith and love without actually "seeing" him. Some suggest that this emphasis on "not seeing yet believing" (cf. a similar theme in Jn 20:29) reflects a contrast with Peter's own viewpoint: he *has* seen. But if that idea is present the author does not make a point of it. It is remarkable how infrequently the New Testament—except for the Johannine tradition—refers to "loving" Jesus (cf. 1 Cor 16:22; Eph 6:24). The thrust of the New Testament perspective (a perspective on the whole shared by 1 Peter) is *through Jesus* to the Father. But here the person of Jesus himself, as the agent of God's salvation, commands the love and loyalty of the believer. Love of Jesus is not repeated in so many words in the rest of the letter, but characteristic of 1 Peter is an emphasis on the *example* of Jesus, especially in his passion (cf. 2:21-25; 3:18-19; 4:1; etc.) and a reverence for the *teaching* of Jesus (cf. 3:9; 4:14; 5:6-7).

The stress on joy is repeated at the end of this segment. Love and trust in Jesus, as well as the experience of God's saving power (v.5), lead to "unutterable and exalted joy." Christian joy wells up from the conviction that our trust in God is reciprocated by his fidelity to us. As verse 9 so forcefully states: the outcome of our faith is that we "carry off" (literally the Greek word used here) the salvation of our souls. By "soul" 1 Peter does not mean our "spiritual soul" in contrast to our material body. The Greek term *"psyche"* used here (and in 1:22; 2:11; 3:20; 4:19) refers to the totality of the human person (body and spirit) as a living, responsible being. Salvation in the bible is considered to be a holistic experience, transforming all of human existence and even the material world in which we live (cf. the sweeping vision of Rom 8:14-39).

WHAT THE PROPHETS ANNOUNCED AND ANGELS LONGED TO SEE BELONGS TO YOU. 1:10-12.

¹⁰The prophets who prophesied of the grace that was to be yours searched and inquired about this salvation; ¹¹they inquired what person or time was indicated by the Spirit of Christ within them when predicting the sufferings of Christ and the subsequent glory. ¹²It was revealed to them that they were serving not themselves but you, in the things which have now been announced to you by those who preached the good news to you through the Holy Spirit sent from heaven, things into which angels long to look.

The thanksgiving section begun in verse 3 is now brought to a close. To this point the author has been directing the attention of the reader to the future, to the glorious salvation provided by God and to the anticipated joy of that salvation experienced even now through a life of faith and love. Now he expands that horizon by tilting their gaze backwards into the past.

The prophets proclaimed the very gift of "grace" that the Christians now experience. Some commentators have interpreted "prophets" to mean not the prophetic voices of the Old Testament but the prophets of the early church who instructed the community on the meaning of Jesus (cf. 1 Cor 14:3-4). That would help explain the mysterious reference to the "Spirit of Christ" in verse 11, but in view of the contrast intended between the words of the prophets (vv. 10-11) and the proclamation of the gospel (v. 12) it is preferable to interpret the "prophets" as the prophetic utterances of the Old Testament. The inspired prophets and other great teachers in Israel directed their message to the contemporary needs of the Jews as God's people. As such the Old Testament scriptures have a message in their own right and not just as a prologue to or prediction of the future. But the purpose of 1 Peter in this passage is to help the Christians see how their gift of faith fits into the entire sweep of salvation history. The Old Testament itself is future-oriented: calling the people of Israel to fidelity and hope as they moved toward the fullness of salvation. Sensing this future orientation and convinced that the dreams of Israel come true in Jesus, many of the New Testament writers looked upon the Old Testament as a prophecy of what was now coming to pass in the experience of the christian community.

This perspective suffuses our passage. The author pictures the prophets (by which he probably means not only the classical prophets but all of the biblical authors) as searching for and inquiring about the salvation which Christians now experience. They were driven to this by "the Spirit of Christ within them." The precise meaning of this phrase is difficult to discern. Does the author mean the Spirit in a general sense, that is, the Spirit of God that gave the prophets insight into God's plan of salvation? Or, as the words literally say, were they driven by *Christ's* own Spirit, by a mysterious presence of Christ at work even before his incarnation? The latter seems to be the meaning of the text. Not unlike the prologue to John's Gospel (Jn 1:1-18) the author seems to affirm a mysterious pre-existence of Jesus at work in the world guiding it to the climax of salvation history.

The Spirit of Christ led the prophets to predict the very heart of the gospel: his death and resurrection. The pattern of suffering leading to glory is constantly alluded to in the letter because, for the author, it describes the essence of the christian vocation (cf. below 2:19-25; 3:18; 4:1-2,13; 5:10).

The author considers the prophecy of salvation to be a "service" for the Christians. How this service was "revealed" to the prophets (v.12) is not made clear. But now these "things" (the predicted salvation) have been communicated to the Christians by those who preached the gospel (literally, the "good news"). The power to proclaim the Gospel is itself the work of the Holy Spirit, a conviction that 1 Peter shares with many other New Testament traditions.

The cosmic scope of salvation history is evoked even more in the final words of verse 12. With touching imagery the author exclaims that the angels "longed to look at" (literally "longed to bend over and peer into") the beautiful life of salvation which God, through the agency of the Spirit, has given to the Christians. 1 Peter cannot conceal his sheer joy and pride in being a Christian.

A CALL TO HOLINESS.
1:13-16.

> 13Therefore gird up your minds, be sober, set your hope fully upon the grace that is coming to you at the revelation of Jesus Christ. 14As obedient children, do not be conformed to the passions of your former ignorance, 15but as he who called you is holy, be holy yourselves in all your conduct; 16since it is written, "You shall be holy, for I am holy."

Having scanned the foundations of christian existence in the triumphant blessing section (1:2-12), the author now turns to the immediate purpose of his letter: an exhortation to live a holy life. The sequence is not without significance. The epistle does not begin with moral demands necessary for the Christians to be worthy of their vocation. Rather, in a pattern often used in Paul's epistles, the reverse is the case: only after strongly affirming the beauty and the power of their christian vocation does the author proceed to the demands of living it out; first the good news, then a search for the appropriate response to the gospel (note the emphatic "therefore" in v. 13). The exhortations begun here will continue to the end of the first major division of the letter in 2:10. These first few verses (13-16) stress the call to "holiness."

The opening verse (13) begins with a "journey" image, reflecting the "exile" status of the readers (cf. 1:1). Literally they are to "hitch up the waists of your minds"—a call for readiness as they set out towards the "grace," the full experience of salvation, that will be theirs at the completion of human history. The demand to be "sober" (cf. also 5:8) and the reference to active "hope" are a typical blend of thought found throughout this epistle. The difficulty of living a gospel life in a world filled with alien values is never discounted; however, the cost of discipleship results not in grim endurance but in active hope. The "belt" image and the call to a life of active and alert discipleship echo a number of gospel sayings (cf. Lk 12:35; Jn 21:18).

The call to live a life of hope is now repeated in other images. The Christians, as children of God through the rebirth of baptism, should be "obedient," totally responsive not to "the passions of their former ignorance" but to the "holy" God who called them into a life of hope. Both Jewish and early christian literature indicted the pagans for their "ignorance" of God (cf. Rom 1:18-32). This ignorance was deepened by the pagans' indulgence of their "passions" or unsound desires. The author will cite a stock list of these kinds of "desires" in 4:3—licentiousness, drunkenness, lawless idolatry, etc. These are the symptoms of despair, signs of a life without hope or meaning. Peter writes to Christians who had once been part of that world ("your former ignorance") but now are born to a new life. The goal of that life is "holiness" because the One to whom they are drawn is holy. Note that the author does not describe "holiness" as withdrawal from the world but as the transformation of their "conduct" (literally their "way of life," perhaps another touch of the journey imagery). As later passages will make clear (cf. 2:11-12), 1 Peter wants holiness to be a manifest witness for the sake of a world without God.

A citation from Leviticus 19:2 "you shall be holy, for I am holy" punctuates this call to holiness and gives it the authority of the scriptures, a device used by the author in a number of exhortation passages (cf. 2:3; 3:10; 4:18; 5:5).

FEAR BEFORE A GOD OF HOPE.
1:17-21.

[17]And if you invoke as Father him who judges each one impartially according to his deeds, conduct yourselves with fear throughout the time of your exile. [18]You know that you were ransomed from the futile ways inherited from your fathers, not with perishable things such as silver or gold, [19]but with the precious blood of Christ, like that of a lamb without blemish or spot. [20]He was destined before the foundation of the world but was made manifest at the end of the times for your sake. [21]Through him you have confidence in God, who raised him from the dead and gave him glory, so that your faith and hope are in God.

The invitation to a transformed life of holiness continues with new imagery. The gift of christian life in baptism brings with it the ability to invoke God as our "Father" (cf. Rom 8:15-17 where Paul states this same conviction). But this Father remains the awesome God who is the author of all life, the totally other, the Holy One who completely transcends the limits of human life. Ultimately all human life originates with him and is responsible to him. This line of reflection moves our author from the theme of "holiness" to that of "fear" of God as judge. Since the newborn life of the Christian is destined for God and is bound up with God, that life (literally "each one's work") will be impartially evaluated by God. Therefore the Christian cannot take his or her call to holiness casually. Our sojourn in "exile," our way of discipleship, must be shot through with "fear" of God. The whole tenor of 1 Peter (and, in fact, the entire New Testament) does not mean "fear" in the sense of anxious trembling before a vengeful God. The mood is that of reverence or awe before the mystery of God and the overwhelming compassion he freely shows us. An attitude of reverence has marked biblical piety from Moses to Jesus and is not incompatible with confident trust in God's love (as 1 Peter will conclude in v.21).

Verse 18 opens with an emphatic "you know . . ." and then proceeds to a string of images describing God's saving act through Jesus. Some scholars suggest that the images which follow the "you know" may be snatches of hymns and liturgical prayers known to the Christians of Asia Minor. 1 Peter cites them here to bring his call to holiness back to the foundation on which it rests.

The first of these images is that of "ransom": the "precious blood of Christ" has ransomed Christians from a life of futility. This metaphor for redemption is also found in Mark 10:45 as a saying of Jesus: "For the Son of Man also came not to be served but to serve, and to give his life as a ransom for many" (cf. also 1 Tim 2:6). The biblical origin of this ransom metaphor is probably Isaiah 53:10-12 where the Suffering Servant, a mysterious redemptive figure, atones for the sins of Israel by bearing its pain and suffering. Early christian theology portrayed Jesus as the perfect embodiment of this representative figure: through the suffering, death and resurrection of Jesus, humanity has been rescued from the slavery of sin and death. It would be a distortion of biblical thought to push this metaphor too far by filling out the drama and making God the vindictive slave master who demands the price of Jesus' blood in order to release his captives. The focus of the metaphor is solely on the saving effect of Jesus' death and resurrection—we are "ransomed," redeemed by him; the rest of the scenario is left undeveloped.

What we are ransomed from is described as "the futile ways inherited from your fathers." The journey image cited in verse 15 is repeated, but now it describes an aimless wandering that comes as an inheritance of despair from previous generations. There is a realistic assessment of the social nature of sin in this phrase (not unlike Paul's description of sin in Romans 5:12-21).

In connection with the ransom image, the author speaks of Jesus as "a lamb without blemish or spot." Isaiah 53:7 speaks of the Servant figure as a "lamb" who silently submits to shearing or slaughter. Although this Servant allusion may be intended by our author, his use of the term "without blemish or spot" suggests that he wishes to describe Jesus as the *Passover* Lamb. According to the ritual laid down in chapter 12 of Exodus, the slaughter of a lamb "without blemish" (Ex 12:5) celebrated the rescue of Israel from slavery. Paul explicitly calls Jesus "our Paschal Lamb" in 1 Corinthians 5:7 and the reference to Jesus' being spared the breaking of his legs at the moment of death according to John 19:36 (citing Ex 12:46) comes from the same tradition. (Jesus is also called "Lamb of God" in Jn 1:29 and 1:35 and "the Lamb who was slain" in the Apocalypse).

The same cosmic sweep of history that erupted in verses 10-12 seems to re-emerge, this time in a fragment of a hymn or poetry about Jesus himself. He was "destined" (literally "known beforehand" by God) before the world was created but was "made manifest" at the climax of world history in which the Christians are lucky enough to be alive. As in the reference to the "Spirit of Christ" in verse 11, the author affirms the pre-existence of Christ. Jewish thought (as, for example, I Henoch 62:7, a work roughly contemporary with 1 Peter) speculated that the great heroes of Israel were somehow enjoying a hidden existence in the mind of God from the very beginning of the plan of salvation. A similar idea is expressed here about Jesus.

Although this segment began by calling for fear (17) it ends with a re-affirmation of confidence and hope (21). Through Jesus, because of his death and resurrection on our behalf, we have "confidence" (literally, "faith" or trust) in God. The same God who brought Jesus from death to glory is the one in whom we place our trust and on whom we rest our hope. In verse 13, the opening verse of the entire exhortation section, the Christians were asked to hitch up their belts and set out hopefully for the day of the Lord. The goal of that journey is invoked again; our trust and hope are, literally, "towards God."

LOVE ONE ANOTHER EARNESTLY FROM THE HEART.
1:22-2:3.

> [22]Having purified your souls by your obedience to the truth for a sincere love of the brethren, love one another earnestly from the heart. [23]You have been born anew, not of perishable seed but of imperishable, through the living and abiding word of God; [24]for
> "All flesh is like grass
> and all its glory like the flower of grass.
> The grass withers, and the flower falls,
> [25]but the word of the Lord abides for ever."
> That word is the good news which was preached to you.
> 2   So put away all malice and all guile and insincerity and envy and all slander. [2]Like newborn babes, long for the pure spiritual milk, that by it you may grow up to salvation; [3]for you have tasted the kindness of the Lord.

This passage inaugurates a pattern repeated throughout the letter; a series of directives or exhortations concerning holiness crescendo in an appeal for mutual love within the community (cf. 3:8-12; 4:8-11; 5:5). This pattern harmonizes with the basic theology of the letter: 1) through baptism the Christian is made part of God's people—christian existence is a communal existence (cf. 2:9-10) and, therefore, 2) the love that unites God's people is one of its most effective means of witness to the world (2:9, 11; 4:11).

The call to "love one another earnestly from the heart" is based on the very nature of christian existence. Their "souls," their very selves (cf. comments under 1:9), have been "purified by... obedience to the truth." "Obedience to the truth" means a life of faith, a life totally responsive to the ultimate truth of God's love. In 1:2 and 1:14 the author uses "obedience" in the same sense. This total response to God's love has the effect of purifying one's life from the self-indulgent and dead-ended desires that make human life shallow (cf 1:14). Being open to God's love means leading a life that is now capable of "sincere love of the brethren" ("brethren" being a quasi-technical term for all the members of the christian community).

1 Peter puts the term "purified" in the past tense and it is likely that he is thinking of the act of baptism as the purifying act which signified their conversion of heart from egoism to love. That becomes more evident in verse 27 where he repeats the same ideas but now in the imagery of "re-birth" (cf. 1:3). Baptism marks the turning away from a life of futility (cf. 1:14, 18) to a new life of hope. The author is not, of course, talking merely about the ritual act of baptism as such but has in mind the entire effect of God's grace on the human person, an effect that is signified in the single act of baptism. Thus he points to the power of "the living and abiding word of God" as the impulse for this new life of the Christian. The "word" is a metaphor for God himself, for the sustaining force of his saving presence. This "abiding" of the word is what is emphasized by the quotation from Isaiah 40:6-8 in verse 24. That word of God is identified with the "good news" or "gospel" which the Christians had preached to them and which ultimately led them to conversion and baptism.

In effect, the author points to sincere "love of one another from the heart" as the sign of authentic conversion, a basic tenet of the entire New Testament. This is repeated with another set of metaphors in the first three verses of chapter 2. The Christian should "take off" the old ways of sin as if they were a filthy set of clothes (an image found in Rom 13:12; Col 3:8; Eph 4:22,25 and Jas 1:21). This might reflect the ancient baptismal ritual in which the candidates stripped before entering the water. The list of vices—"all malice," "all guile," "insincerity," "envy," and "all slander"—does not seem to refer to specific problems in the communities for whom the letter is written. In fact, the letter's silence on any kind of internal dissension or errors within these

churches makes it an exception within the New Testament.
In the letters of Paul and in most of the other New Testament books some of the specific failings of the christian
community are glaring. The vices listed here (cf. also 4:3)
seem to be of a very general nature and are typical of the
stock lists of sins found in other New Testament texts
(cf. Rom 1:29; 2 Cor 12:20; Eph 4:31; Col 3:8). However, the
sins mentioned are the kind that poison human relationships
and that is the point at issue.

The stripping away of sin is only one side of the conversion
process; the plunge into new life is the other. So verse 2 in-
vites the Christians as "newborn babes" to "long for the pure
spiritual milk that by it you may grow up to salvation." The
image of "newborn babes" builds on the baptismal metaphor
of rebirth cited in 1:23. The abiding word of God, the gospel
preached to them, is an invitation to a new life. That life
begins as a process of growth which leads toward the fulness
of salvation. This harmonizes with the journey imagery used
in 1:13-21 and with the call to perseverance through trial
in 1:3-9. In all of these texts 1 Peter conceives of christian
life not as an instant and easily attained experience but as a
life-long process of growth towards the full beauty of our
humanity. In 1 Corinthians 3:1-3 and in Hebrews 5:12-14 the
metaphor of milk for the newborn is used with a pejorative
tone; weak and immature Christians get only milk in contrast to the hearty diet of the fully developed believer. But in
1 Peter "milk" is not a grudging concession to weakness, but
a hope-filled sign of God's nourishment intended for those
who grow towards maturity.

An allusion to Psalm 34:8 ("O taste and see that the Lord
is good!") rounds out the passage. The Christians *have tasted*
the kindness of the Lord; they have already experienced the
amazing goodness and compassion of God through the
redemptive work of Jesus' death and resurrection (1:18-21)
and by their baptismal call to a new life of love and hope
(1:22-25). This *experience* gives them the motivation to continue in the process of salvation. Psalm 34 is quoted in the
writings of the Qumran community and in Hebrews 6:4-5 in

reference to religious experience. Here as in many other places in the letter, our author draws on a wide range of traditional imagery. The title "lord" may apply here to Jesus, the one through whom God's life has come to us (cf. 1:21). Although the original psalm used the title of Yahweh, the opening verse of the next section (cf. 2:4) definitely speaks of Jesus ("come to him") and seems to build on the "Lord" reference in 2:3.

THE CHURCH: A TEMPLE OF LIVING STONE, A COVENANT PEOPLE.
2:4-10.

The next seven verses are the final segment in the first major division of 1 Peter (1:2–2:10); we have entitled this whole division "The Foundation of Christian Existence." This concluding passage is considered by many to be the most substantial description of christian life in 1 Peter, indeed one without peer in the entire New Testament. Up to this point the author has braided together references to God's merciful act of salvation with allusions to baptism and to the responsibilities of converted Christians. In the immediately preceeding passage (1:22–2:13) he had stressed the communal nature of christian existence and pleaded for a community of love. The story of salvation and the call to be a people erupt again in this stirring description of what it means to be a church.

Two basic images—that of "stone" and that of election or covenant—dominate the passage. The author develops these basic images by means of biblical quotes and metaphors. The whole passage is stitched together like a vivid patchwork quilt that presents a stunning image of the church. Some scholars suggest that the author borrowed most of this material (especially vv.4-5 and 9-10) from an early christian hymn. But there is no real evidence for this. Although the images of stone and covenant were obviously employed by Jewish and christian tradition prior to this epistle, 1 Peter can claim credit for the form they take here.

THE IMAGE OF STONE.
2:4-8.

> [4]Come to him, to that living stone, rejected by men but in God's sight chosen and precious; [5]and like living stones be yourselves built into a spiritual house, to be a holy priesthood, to offer spiritual sacrifices acceptable to God through Jesus Christ. [6]For it stands in scripture:
> "Behold, I am laying in Zion a stone,
> a cornerstone chosen and
> precious,
> and he who believes in him will not
> be put to shame."
> [7]To you therefore who believe, he is precious, but for those who do not believe,
> "The very stone which the builders
> rejected
> has become the head of the corner,"
> [8]and
> "A stone that will make men
> stumble,
> a rock that will make them fall";
> for they stumble because they disobey the word, as they were destined to do.

The symbol of "stone" or "rock" is used with a variety of meanings in both the Old and New Testaments. One basic meaning develops the idea of *foundation stone.* According to a mythology current in several ancient Near Eastern cultures, the creation of the world began with the laying of a foundation stone marking the center of the universe. This stone capped the chaotic waters of the subterranean seas and became the starting point for construction of the rest of the world. Usually the sacred capital city and its temple are said to have been built on this hub. Such mythology is detectable in the quotation from Isaiah 28:16 which 1 Peter cites in 2:6. Mount Zion on which Jerusalem and its temple are built is the site of this cosmic cornerstone: it is thus a sure and unshakable foundation for God's people.

Another dimension of the stone symbol is that of *obstacle* or stumbling stone. The stone stands immovably in the way, an image of strength and challenge in adversity. This image is applied to God in Isaiah 8:14, a text cited in verse 8 of our passage.

The third facet of this stone symbol seems to combine foundation stone and stumbling stone. Psalm 118:22 uses the metaphor of a stone that is rejectd by the builders yet becomes the cornerstone of the building. In the psalm this image is applied to the plight of the psalmist who seems to express his thanksgiving for victory in battle. The king (or whoever the psalmist may represent) was rejected by his people but with God's help has prevailed over the enemy.

Each of the stone images is utilized by the New Testament as the early Christians re-interpreted biblical symbols to apply them to their own experience. The image of foundation stone seems to be one influence on Matthew 16:18 where Jesus declares Peter to be the "rock" on which he will build his new community. Closer to the sense of 1 Peter, however, is Ephesians 2:20-22. Here Jesus himself is the cornerstone or foundation stone and the edifice that is constructed is a "holy temple in the Lord; in whom you also are built into it for a dwelling place of God in the Spirit." This links together foundation stone and the temple building, a link already present in the ancient mythology and in Isaiah 28:16. The Jewish reformers at Qumran used the same Isaiah text and applied it to their community as God's house (in the Manual of Discipline and The Book of Hymns). The idea that the risen Jesus becomes the personification of the temple is strongly affirmed in John 2:19-22 ("destroy this temple and in three days I will raise it up") and in Mark 14:58 ("destroy this temple that is made with hands, and in three days I will build another not made with hands"). The extension of the temple image to the Christians themselves is made by Ephesians and 1 Peter.

The theme of the "rejected cornerstone" is also found in the New Testament. Mark cites Psalm 118:22 as a commentary on the meaning of the parable of the vineyard

(Mk 12:10-11). Both the lightly concealed allegory of the parable and the psalm quote refer to the death and resurrection of Jesus. Matthew (21:42) follows Mark faithfully in this but Luke (20:17-18) expands the quote from the psalm by adding the image of the stumbling block from Isaiah 8:14. For those who reject Jesus he is an obstacle and a sign of judgement but for those who accept him he is a precious cornerstone. Thus Luke combines themes and Old Testament quotations just as 1 Peter does. This is a sure sign that these images for Jesus and the church were already in circulation before either Luke or 1 Peter put them in writing.

Having reviewed the diverse use of the stone symbol, we can now turn to the text of 1 Peter 2:4-8. The whole section begins with an invitation: "Come to him." The author has spoken of Jesus Christ as both the inauguration and the culmination of the process of salvation. The death and resurrection of Jesus was the saving act that gave birth to living hope (1:3). Even before the foundation of the world Jesus was present in the mind of God (1:20); his Spirit moved the prophets to prepare the way of salvation (1:11). And the target of that journey is the full revelation of Jesus (1:13) at the completion of the world. As the Christians are on their way, they love their Lord without seeing him, they trust in him and rejoice (1:8). All of these previous statements about the relationship of Jesus and the Christians were summed up in 2:3—"you have tasted the kindness of the Lord." This testimony to the central role of Jesus in christian experience gives an urgency to the plea: "Come to him." The Christians are invited to plunge fully into the way of salvation, to live out their baptismal call. The warm inviting tone of the opening phrase is reminiscent of the saying of Jesus in Matthew 11:28—"Come to me, all you who labor and are heavy laden, and I will give you rest."

The introduction of the stone imagery causes a slight mixing of metaphors: the invitation to *come* to a "living *stone*, rejected by men but in God's sight chosen and precious" (2:4). This description of Jesus draws on two of the symbolic uses of stone we have discussed above. Jesus is both the foundation stone as affirmed by the quote of Isaiah 28:16 in verse 6 and a rejected cornerstone as illustrated in the quote of Psalm 118:22 in verse 7. The Christians are invited to base their life of discipleship on Jesus himself; to find in him the confidence needed for their christian witness (as in 1:21). He is a *living* stone, one who in spite of rejection and death has been raised up by God. Perhaps the most insistent message of 1 Peter is the pattern of death-resurrection: for Jesus himself and for the Christians who trust in him. Suffering for the sake of the gospel is a redemptive act (cf. the discussion under 2:21-25).

The bond between Jesus "the living stone" and the Christians brings life to them: in verse 5 the community itself is labeled "living stones." By building their lives and their community on the foundation of Jesus the Christians are constructed into "a spiritual house." Although some scholars have questioned this, it seems most probable that by "house" 1 Peter means the *temple*. The following phrases speak of "priesthood" and "sacrifices." Thus, as in Ephesians 2:20-22, the christian community is now designated as a living temple. The Jerusalem temple was a central institution of Jewish life. Here Yahweh was present to his people in a unique way. Here was the center of Israel's worship and the seat of its teaching, the taproot of its identity as a covenant people. Now 1 Peter, drawing on a theological tradition already present in the church (in addition to Eph 2:20-22, cf. 1 Cor 3:16-17; 2 Cor 6:16; 1 Tim 3:15; Heb 3:6) applies that sacred name to a community of people. The temple is no longer a building or an institution but a living community. Here is where God is present and where true worship is offered to him. Therefore the Christians form "a holy priesthood" (a name for Israel in Ex 19:6 and Is 61:6), that is, they are the custodians and leaders in this living temple. To be part of a sacred place required "holiness" (cf. 1:13-16). And it also requires a life of service which the author states in temple language: offering "spiritual sacrifices acceptable to God through Jesus Christ." The language bears careful analysis. By "spiritual sacrifices" the author does not mean simply "spiritual" as opposed to the "material" or animal and grain sacrifices of the Jewish temple liturgy. Rather the sense of "spiritual" here is that the sacrifices offered to God come from the totality of the human person; they are not merely external acts but spring from a committed heart. This theme is not a Christian invention but was a recurrent motif in Israel itself. Psalm 51:17 proclaims that "the sacrifice acceptable to God is a broken spirit; a broken and contrite heart, O God, thou wilt not despise" (cf. also Ps 69:30-33; 141:2). The prophets challenged the leaders of Israel on the hypocrisy of liturgical worship that coexisted with deeds of injustice (cf. the powerful text of Is 1:10-20). And during the turbulent period of the first century A.D. both the Pharisees and the Essenes (the reform group represented at Qumran) reminded the people that sincere obedience to the law was a form of acceptable sacrifice. Thus to be a holy priesthood offering sacrifices in God's new temple does not mean withdrawal into some sacred zone but is a plea for a life fully convinced of its sacredness and fully committed to action.

1 Peter describes the "temple" not as a static reality but as under construction, "being built up." The *process* of conversion and growth discussed in 2:2 is acknowledged again. Paul speaks similarly of "building up" the church in 1 Corinthians 14:12. Ephesians 4:11-12 cites the various ministries in the community and says that the purpose of these "gifts" is "to equip the saints . . . for building up the body of Christ." The building up of the church as a living temple is an ongoing process, a "way" of discipleship.

Verses 7 and 8 add a final comment on the stone symbol. For the believers, Christ is indeed the precious foundation stone on which they base their new life. But for those who reject Jesus and the gospel, who choose a life of futility, this "stone" becomes the "stumbling stone." Although both Psalm 118:22 and Isaiah 8:14 are quoted, it is the mood of the latter which dominates. Those who experience God's judgement are not unbelievers in general but those who "disobey the word, as they were destined to do so." The word of God, the gospel, was the impulse of new life for the Christians (1:24-25). Their "obedience" to their truth helped them shed a life of meaningless indulgence (1:22; 2:1) and set them on the way of salvation. But those to whom the gospel is offered yet who reject it have invited death into their lives. 1 Peter (as does all the New Testament) does not consider encounter with the gospel a casual affair; it is a matter of life or death. In this sense, the person of Jesus (as proclaimed by the word and witness of the community) stands as an immovable rock in the flow of human history. Those whose God-given destiny brings them into knowing contact with it must either cling to it and build their lives upon it, or if they deliberately choose, attempt to skirt that rock and ignore it. To choose the latter course is fatal; they will trip and fall. The deep conviction that the proclamation of the gospel offers the way to genuine human life underwrites the mission thrust of the rest of the epistle.

THE IMAGE OF COVENANT.
2:9-10.

> ⁹But you are a chosen race, a royal priesthood, a holy nation, God's own people, that you may declare the wonderful deeds of him who called you out of darkness into his marvelous light. ¹⁰Once you were no people but now you are God's people; once you had not received mercy but now you have received mercy.

Once again our author rummages through the treasure chest of Old Testament symbols to find ones that are just right for describing what it means to be the church. This time he chooses the image of covenant and election. The solemn treaty drawn up between Yahweh and Israel is the very heart of biblical Judaism. This pact sealed Israel's election as God's own people. Although the covenant took many forms in the legal codes of the ancient Near East, it was basically a contract between a powerful king and lesser

vassal states. It was a mutual pledge of loyalty and protection. In the patriarchal narratives a number of covenants
were struck between God and Israel, such as the covenant
with Noah (Gen 9:1-19) and with Abraham (Gen 15:1-2).
But the archetype of all biblical covenants was the great
covenant between Yahweh and Moses at Sinai during the
Exodus. Later biblical authors would draw on this pledge
between God and Israel in order to recall God's promised
fidelity or to challenge Israel for its failures. Some traditions
such as Jeremiah or Ezekiel would speak of Israel's hope for
final peace and redemption as a great covenant renewal, a
new covenant carved not in stone but in the "fleshy tablets
of the heart" (Jer 31:33; Ezek 11:19).

It is not surprising that the early Christians re-interpreted
this great biblical symbol in the light of their faith in Jesus.
He himself was God's pledge of love and fidelity to Israel.
His death and resurrection forged the new covenant (cf.
Mk 14:24; Lk 22:20; 1 Cor 11:25). The church was the new
covenant people, heirs to the promises made to Israel.
1 Peter thus draws on a theme that was already part of early
christian self-understanding. In using texts associated with
covenant and election the author seems to evoke two moods:
one the triumphant sense of election as God's people as
described in Exodus 19 and Isaiah 43, the other, the muted,
sadder-but-wiser covenant renewal spoken of by Hosea 1-2.
Using these two traditions the epistle portrays the church as
it really is: chosen yet itself capable of failure; its wounds
barely healed, yet sent into the world to proclaim God's
greatness.

Verse 9 opens with a contrast: "But *you . . .*" The previous
verses (4-8) recalled both God's choice or election of the
Christians and the tragedy of those who refuse the invitation
of the gospel. These latter seem destined for failure but
those who accept God's good news are chosen for new life.

A string of powerful names are given to the Christians as
God's people. Some of these come from Exodus 19:6, part of
the triumphant Sinai covenant text spoken of above. 1 Peter
enriches this text with quotations from Isaiah 43:20-21, a

passage pointed toward a future renewal of the covenant. The first phrase—"a chosen race"—comes from the Isaiah text (43:20) and captures the basic mood that 1 Peter wants to convey. The Christians are "chosen," they belong to God, they are his people. This consciousness is the basis for hope and the source of the christian mission.

A second phrase builds on the first. They are "a royal priesthood." Here our author dips into Exodus 19:6, quoting literally from the Septuagint, the Greek translation of the Old Testament used by the early Christians. The accuracy of translating this phrase as "royal priesthood" has been challenged. The Greek word *Basileion* here rendered as the adjective "royal" is almost always a *noun* in biblical Greek and, in fact, in the original Hebrew text of Exodus 19:6 there is no adjective but a noun. Thus not "royal" but a "kingly house" or "royal residence." Apocalypse 1:6 and 5:10 allude to this Exodus text and speak of the community as "a kingdom" and as "priests"—accurately translating the two nouns. For these reasons an increasing number of modern scholars believe this phrase in 1 Peter contains two separate descriptions of the church: "a royal residence" (i.e., "a house of kings") and "priesthood" or "a community of priests." Both phrases fit into 1 Peter's collage of images. In 2:5 he already spoke of the community as "a spiritual house," a temple. In 4:17 the church will be named "the household of God." Now it is called "a royal house." All these labels are justified because of the author's conviction that God and his Spirit are present and at work in the christian community. The image of the Christians as "priests" was also spoken of in 2:5. Because the church is God's temple the members of the community are chosen to be in God's presence, to reflect his holiness and to be active in worship and service on God's behalf. Both of these "priestly" labels for the church (2:5 and 2:9) have been the focus of an often tense debate in post-reformation Christianity. Some consider these texts as the basis for a "priesthood of believers" which, in effect, would deny the possibility of a specific priestly ministry in the church. But the author of this letter was not a party to the later debate. In speaking of a "priesthood" exercised by all Christians he was neither affirming or denying the possibility of a specific liturgical ministry in the church, just as the author of Exodus 19 could speak of the entire Israelite community as "priestly" without thereby passing judgement on the Levitical priesthood. The positive contribution of these texts in 1 Peter is that they affirm the dignity and responsibility of each Christian who, by baptism, is called to worship God and to be dedicated to his service in the world. The epistle does not address (and therefore can hardly solve) the question of an ordained priesthood.

Two more descriptive phrases from Exodus 19 and Isaiah 43 drive home the community's sense of being chosen by God. In the words of Exodus 19:6 they are a "holy nation." The word "nation" accurately picks up the connotation of the Greek word *ethnos* which 1 Peter uses here. The Christians in Rome, Pontus, Galatia, Cappadocia and Bithynia (1:1) had differing ethnic roots. But their common calling as Christians cut through the frontiers of culture and history and gave them a sense of common identity. They had all been touched by God; they were "holy," sacred. They were a global community. A final title directly trumpets their *chosen* status. In the words of Isaiah 43:21 the Christians are "God's own people." Literally the text says "a people for [God's] possession." The Greek word *laos*, "people," is the term most frequently used in the bible to describe Israel as a community whose life and destiny are bound up with God. In applying these sacred titles to the church, the Christians were recognizing their place in God's mysterious plan of salvation. Out of love Yahweh had chosen the Israelites, an insignificant people (cf. Dt 7:6-8) to be the bearers of his promises to humanity. In spite of failure and tragedy Israel never lost that conviction. The early Christians now see themselves as part of that incredible heritage. It is remarkable that 1 Peter, in contrast to almost every other New Testament writing, does not play off the elect status of the Christians against Israel's rejection of the gospel. The epistle reflects none of the Jewish-Gentile polarity that was a dominant concern of Paul and the gospel literature.

The author's stress on the church's identity as a chosen covenant people is not in a spirit of chest-thumping arrogance or smug assurance. The Christians are chosen not to savor their own good fortune but to be sent out on mission. They are to "declare the wonderful deeds of him who called you out of darkness into his marvelous light." The first half of this statement seems to be a paraphrase of Isaiah 43:21 ("the people whom I formed for myself that *they might declare my praise*"). 1 Peter uses the technical term "evangelize" (literally, "proclaim the good news") in place of Isaiah's more general term "declare." This is the christian mission: to announce to the world the "wonderful deeds," the loving acts of salvation that God intends on behalf of humanity. As the epistle has repeatedly noted, the Christians themselves have experienced these "wonderful deeds." They have been "called out of darkness into God's own marvelous light" (a common metaphor for conversion in the New Testament and the early Fathers of the church). In previous verses this had been described as a "new birth" (1:3,23), as a rescue from a life of futility (1:14,18). Therefore, "preaching the gospel" is not some canned propaganda, but the living testimony of a people who have been touched by God and who can show the results in their own lives. This testimony will be the primary concern of 1 Peter in the next major section of the epistle (cf. 2:11).

In verse 10 our author turns to the rich theology of Hosea in a last effort to describe the mystery of the church. A re-reading of this remarkable prophet, especially chapters 1 and 2 (the source of the quotations in 1 Pt 2:10), is necessary in order to catch the flavor of the text. Hosea recasts the mood of covenant theology by reflecting on the bond between God and Israel in the light of his own experience of a broken marriage. Gomer, his wife, apparently a former prostitute at a Canaanite pagan shrine, repeatedly leaves Hosea to return to her trade. However, neither her constant infidelity nor even the illegitimate children she bears (wryly named "No-pity" and "Not-my-people," cf. Hos 1:6-9) could cure the prophet of his love for her. That love—scorned, tested, filled with pain yet unbreakable—gave Hosea a glimpse of the way Yahweh loved Israel. The "harlot Israel" is pursued by a God who madly loves her in spite of shame and infidelity (Hos 3:1). In chapter 2 Hosea uses one of the most breathtaking descriptions of God's love in all of biblical literature to portray the renewal of the covenant as Yahweh's final seduction of his wandering lady (cf. especially 2:14-23). 1 Peter selects the final verse of this passage to complete his word portrait of the church. Once the Christians were "no people" caught in a dizzy merry-go-round of self-seeking (cf. 1:14,18; 2:1; 4:3-4). But now they are caught up in God's embrace and have become his people. Once they had experienced "no-mercy"—lives out of touch with God, lives without hope. But now they have tasted God's goodness.

The Hosea text injects the right hue into 1 Peter's portrait of the church. This is not a community of angels nor some doe-eyed band of innocents. They are people who have come home after a long and troubled absence. They are a sadder-but-wiser church, more likely to look with compassion on a broken world because they had been there themselves.

Part II.

The Church in the World:

Participate, Be Free!

2:11 – 4:11.

No New Testament book was written simply to speculate on the meaning of christian faith. The primary goal is to urge Christians to *live* their faith. 1 Peter is no exception. Now that his beautiful word-portrait of the church and the christian vocation has been completed, the author concentrates on urging the Christians to *be* that church in the world. Even in the previous section 1 Peter could not refrain from giving advice. The Christians were urged to rejoice, to be sober and watchful, to be holy, to reverence God, to love one another, to rest their lives on Jesus. But these urgent pleas were quick probes in passages which concentrated primarily on reminding the Christians *who* they were as God's people. Now the author gives full attention to *what* God's people should *do*.

FREEDOM AND RESPONSIBILITY.
2:11-12.

> [11]Beloved, I beseech you as aliens and exiles to abstain from the passions of the flesh that wage war against your soul. [12]Maintain good conduct among the Gentiles, so that in case they speak against you as wrongdoers, they may see your good deeds and glorify God on the day of visitation.

One catches the author's own awareness of moving to a new phase in his letter in the opening words of verse 11. He addresses the Christians as "beloved," an expression that is no mere cliche. In 1:22 Peter had urged the believers "to love one another earnestly from the heart." Every Christian has been born anew; each one is a sacred creation of God, a living stone in God's living temple. This is the "truth" that leads to "a sincere love of the brethren" (cf. also 1:22). And 1 Peter recalls the opening line of his letter when he again addresses his fellow Christians as "aliens" and "exiles." They are aliens or strangers because their values put them at a distance from the pagan society around them. They are exiles because they belong to a world of hope and love that seems far removed from the pagan world in which they are actually immersed.

The author recalls this exile status because he now intends to talk about how one should live in a world intrinsically alien to the gospel. In these first two verses (11-12) 1 Peter lays down basic principles of christian existence. A life based on the gospel demands inner freedom from destructive values but it also means full participation in the world so that the witness of a genuine human life can have its effect. This is a key insight of the letter and gives it perennial significance. An intelligent analysis of his society convinces the author that many of its values and suppositions are in fact opposed to and destructive of the vision of humanity drawn from the gospel. But instead of withdrawing from the world and constructing a germ-free environment for christian life, 1 Peter risks a spirituality *in* the world.

Verse 11 lays down one of the basic principles for this witness spirituality: the Christian must "abstain from the passions of the flesh that wage war against your soul." In 1:14 the author had used the term "the passions of your former ignorance." "Passions" meant those unchecked desires which are symptomatic of a meaningless life. The expression "passions of the flesh" is similar. In speaking of "flesh" the author is not limiting passion to sensuality or sexual excess. "Flesh" as used in the New Testament connotes a whole dimension of human existence—not the body as opposed to the soul, but the limited and egotistical as opposed to the spiritual and self-transcendent potential of our lives. "Passions of the flesh," then, are those dead-ended desires which make us seek ourselves only and ultimately blunt our humanity. These are the desires that "wage war against your soul," that is, destroy our very selves. The author does not give a checklist of such "passions." But a twentieth century Christian bombarded with the advertising myths of eternal youth, of the "me generation," and of countless artificial needs, should have no trouble filling in the blanks.

Some Greek philosophical traditions had used similar language to describe the truly moral life, a life that was wholly intelligent and detached from any human passion. But 1 Peter is not asking for a life insulated from feeling nor are his words the expected and tired moralisms of the religious reformer. In the context of the whole letter, the plea for abstinence from "passion" is a call for *inner freedom*. It echoes many of the sayings of Jesus in the gospel literature which ask the disciple to "lose his life," "to deny himself, " "to sell what he has." Neither in the sayings of Jesus nor in 1 Peter are these demands for grim living. They are invitations to shed those values and desires and styles of living that we know are self-destructive and will ultimately drain our lives of meaning.

But the call for inner freedom is only one side of the coin. Verse 12 lays down the other principle of a witness spirituality. The Christians are to maintain a beautiful way of living so that a non-believer may eventually be enticed to glorify God. Much of the spirit of 1 Peter is compressed into this key verse. The discipline of inner-freedom is not something to be pursued in the controlled limits of a christian ghetto. It is a discipline for mission; their lives transformed by the gospel are to be "among the gentiles." And even though (or perhaps *because*) the values of the gospel will challenge the world and draw its anger (literally, "they will judge your lives to be evil"), this way of life is to be maintained in the hope that truth and goodness will have the last word. It is worth noting that 1 Peter does not explicitly speak of proselytizing here. He is not asking the Christians to assault their neighbors with propaganda. The goal of the christian mission envisaged here has a cosmic ring to it: that the gentiles might glorify God at the final moment of history. The christian church serves the world by nudging it towards the truth, by lifting up a credible testimony to the inherent beauty of human life. As has already been suggested (cf. 1:3-5), this letter's vision of history has a liturgical bent: the author confidently believes that at the culmination of history all of the world will finally break out in a chorus of praise before the glory of an incredibly compassionate God. This vision is not invented by Peter: the same uplifting hope runs through a saying of Jesus in Matthew 5:11—"Let your light so shine before men, that they may see your good works and give glory to your Father who is in heaven."

COMMITMENT IN THE WORLD.
2:13-17.

> [13]Be subject for the Lord's sake to every human institution, whether it be to the emperor as supreme, [14]or to governors as sent by him to punish those who do wrong and to praise those who do right. [15]For it is God's will that by doing right you should put to silence the ignorance of foolish men. [16]Live as free men, yet without using your freedom as a pretext for evil; but live as servants of God. [17]Honor all men. Love the brotherhood. Fear God. Honor the emperor.

The call for inner freedom and for fearless witness sounded in 2:11-12 is now illustrated by a series of reflections on christian life in the world. This reflection begins with a general statement on political involvement (13-17) and then singles out two difficult conflict situations, that of christian servants (18-25) and that of christian wives married to non-christian husbands (3:1-6). A final section cuts across all the roles of the community (3:7–4:11).

The section considered here (2:13-17) stays for a moment on the level of principle: "Be subject for the Lord's sake to every human institution . . ." This injunction has often been misinterpreted and therefore each phrase should be carefully analyzed. The verb "be subject to" seems at first glance to connote a sense of blind conformity. Such a conclusion would take the reader far from 1 Peter's message. The word can be properly decoded only if one keeps in mind the alternative that is being rejected. "Be subject to" is not a counter to "rebel against" (advice not found in any of the New Testament books) but to "withdraw from." In other words, the choice before the Christians who are exiles and strangers in society is either to draw up their wagons in a circle and withdraw from compromising entanglements in society—or to plunge fully into the institutions of society while trying to maintain their integrity. The latter choice is implied in the phrase "be subject to," "participate in." During the period of history current with that of Jesus and the early church there was a tradition of Jewish piety which had chosen a monastic or reclusive form of spirituality. The Essenes, as they were called, were a counter-cultural movement that reacted to the excesses of the Hasmonean Jewish dynasty and to the religious establishment at Jerusalem. Some Essenes founded a monastic community at Qumran. Discovery of a large cache of manuscripts at this site in 1948 electrified the world and has greatly enhanced our knowledge of Judaism in the New Testament period. The Essenes' monastic spirituality also had a counterpart in the later monastic movement of Christianity. Even the theology of a book such as the Apocalypse could be seen as calling for retreat from the world as a prophetic stance against its dehumanizing structures. It would be a caricature to brand the monastic movement and other similar styles of christian piety as world-denying, or as calling for complete withdrawal from all societal responsibility. Nevertheless, an important element of these traditions to this day calls for the creation of a special social environment conducive to christian living. The construction, as it were, of the city of God alongside the human city. But the vision of 1 Peter moves in a very different direction, a direction signaled in the opening words of 2:13 and ratified by the entire theological context of the letter.

One of the reasons for this stance of 1 Peter may be the author's conviction about the course of history. He seems to believe that the consummation of the world is not long in coming (cf. 1:6; 4:7; 5:10). In view of the short span of history that must be endured, the author's advice to his church is that they remain within the social and political situations they were in when they first heard the gospel. Even though the christian vision foresees a world order that can and will be very different they should patiently stay involved in the present world. This is Paul's stance in 1 Corinthians: "Let everyone lead the life which the Lord has assigned to him and in which God has called him" (1 Cor 7:17,20,24). And is probably the meaning behind his own statement on being subject to civil authority in Romans 13.

This eschatological perspective does not reduce the message of 1 Peter (nor of Paul, for that matter) to that of feigning participation merely while waiting out the end. Having a strong vision of what the world can and will look like in the plan of God does not make the present state of the world and our responsibility for it meaningless. Nor does it imply that there is no intrinsic connection between the world as *it is* and the world as we hope it *will be*. This is implicit in the remaining phrases of verse 13. Christians are to "be subject (to participate in) for the Lord's sake to every human institution." Participation in society is not a passive burden but a positive mission. The author speaks of "human institutions"—the word for "institutions" used here is *ktisis*, literally, a "creation." In Greek thought it has the sense of a fundamental structure or institution of human society. But used here in a book steeped in biblical tradition and in direct connection with the phrase "for the Lord's sake," the word *ktisis* or creation picks up a rich connotation which takes it far beyond the functional ring of "institution." The fumbling efforts of human beings to build a societal order does not run counter to the creative intention of God; the urge to build is itself an expression of God's own plan of salvation, it is "for the Lord's sake." Therefore involvement in the world's market place, in its evidently imperfect institutions and creations, is not a dirty task that one takes up with rubber gloves. Involvement in the gritty work of the world is a sacred task; it is a participation in the creative work of God himself. That is why in 2:12 and in other parts of the letter, the author is sure that eventually the world will be moved ("created") to give glory to its Lord. Put another way, the Christians should stay in the situations in which they were called because the good and beautiful world they long for will be molded out of the very imperfect world they now belong to.

His principles stated the author now cites examples of what this involvement implies. The first situations are political. In 2:11-12 we noted that 1 Peter calls for a blend of inner freedom and active witness as the ingredients of a christian life in the world. That two-edged principle is evident here. The Christians as good citizens are to offer proper respect and obedience to their civil leaders, the Roman Emperor and the Governors (the latter would be the ruling officials in the Roman provinces of Asia Minor where the recipients of the letter lived). Both of these officials are described in somewhat ideal terms. The word used for Emperor here is literally, *basileus*, "king," a term that would have sacred connotations for the christian reader. And the Governors are described as those "sent... to punish those who do wrong and to praise those who do right" (v. 14). Punishing the evil and rewarding the good were qualities applied to ideal rulers in Greek thought. Paul singles out the same virtues in Romans 13:3.

"Praise for those who do right" slants the message of the next verse toward the call for active witness. It is God's will that the Christians *do right*, a point already stressed in 2:12. "Doing right," as both Peter and his Christians know full well, does not always mean being the "model citizens" beloved by all. "Doing right" in a society that looks at human life and destiny in a way alien to your own view can lead to ridicule, isolation, and even active persecution. But once again 1 Peter's unshakable optimism dominates the mood; the genuinely good lives of the christian citizens will ultimately silence the "ignorance" of foolish people. "Ignorance" as noted above in 1:14, means the blindness and meaninglessness of a life without God.

The capacity to "do right" depends on one's inner freedom. And so verses 16-17 turn to the other principle of a witness spirituality: "live as free men." The nature of this "freedom" is clear from the phrase to which the author couples it: "live as servants of God." One tastes true freedom in being able to let go of the desires and illusions that erode our humanity and in basing our lives on the compassion of the Lord (cf. above 1:21; 2:4, 2:11). Paul, too, uses this kind of imagery: "But now that you have been set free from sin and have become slaves of God . . ." (Rom 6:22).

The dual basis of 1 Peter's spirituality—inner freedom and active witness—are subtly joined in the remaining verse of this passage (17). The words chosen for each relationship in the spectrum of society and the order in which they are presented shows incisive care on the part of the author. The Christians are to *"honor"* every human person: every human being is to be respected as a creature of God called to a destiny of glory. Even though 1 Peter speaks unhesitatingly of conflict and judgement, a sense of respect for all human beings, Christian or not, pervades the letter (cf. 2:12,18; 3:1,7,9,15). *"Love"* the brotherhood; the members of the christian community are bound together in a unique way and their mutual love must be transparent (cf. 1:22; 3:8; 4:8; 5:5). *"Fear"* God: to the Lord of all life one owes a sense of reverence and awe (2:17-21), a relationship without peer. The relationship to the Emperor comes last—not as the climax to what has been a mounting sense of obligation (honor, love, reverence)—but as a forceful emphasis on putting the Emperor in his place! He is to be *"honored,"* the same obligation owed to *every* human being. As a civil ruler he is to be respected and obeyed, but in no way can the Emperor command the allegiance reserved to God. Because of the difficulty in dating the letter (cf. Introduction), it is impossible to know if 1 Peter intends to directly confront Emperor worship—an aberration that would be a problem for the Christians later in the first century. But it is certainly clear in this verse that "being subject to" the Emperor or being "a good citizen" does not mean the abdication of one's critical faculties. The inner freedom of the Christians helps them see both the obligations and the *limits* of civil participation. That free stance is what aggravates the society around them and becomes the source of much suffering. But for Christians "obedient to the truth" (1:22) there was no other course.

The wisdom in 1 Peter's discussion of civil obligations recalls a saying of Jesus found in the synoptic gospels: "Render to Caesar the things that are Caesar's and to God the things that are God's" (Mk 12:17 and parallels).

THE MISSION OF A CHRISTIAN SERVANT.
2:18-25.

[18]Servants, be submissive to your masters with all respect, not only to the kind and gentle but also to the overbearing. [19]For one is approved if, mindful of God, he endures pain while suffering unjustly. [20]For what credit is it, if when you do wrong and are beaten for it you take it patiently? But if when you do right and suffer for it you take it patiently, you have God's approval. [21]For to this you have been called, because Christ also suffered for you, leaving you an example, that you should follow in his steps. [22]He committed no sin; no guile was found on his lips. [23]When he was reviled, he did not revile in return; when he suffered, he did not threaten; but he trusted to him who judges justly. [24]He himself bore our sins in his body on the tree, that we might die to sin and live to

righteousness. By his wounds you have been healed. [25]For
you were straying like sheep, but have now returned to the
Shepherd and Guardian of your souls.

The principles for christian life discussed in the preceeding passages (2:11-17) are now applied to specific roles
in society: servants (2:18-25), wives (3:1-6), husbands (3:7).
The literary device of directing moral exhortations to
various members of a household was common in Greco-
Roman literature and similar forms are used in other New
Testament books (cf. Col 3:18–4:1 and Eph 5:22–6:9). In
1 Timothy and Titus a list-format is used to describe the
qualities needed for various offices or ministries in the
community. In 1 Peter the list concerns the roles within
society. The author singles out two groups for special attention: servants and wives, especially those married to
non-christian husbands. Of all the Christians living in society, these were the two groups that had to endure the most
painful conflict between their christian freedom and their
efforts to live a good life in the world.

The first segment (18-20) of the passage on servants is
addressed directly to them; the concluding portion (21-25)
hammers out a theology of suffering for the benefit of all
the readers of the letter.

The ones addressed are *oiketoi,* literally, "members of
the household." Since the author does not use the more
technical word *doulos* or "slave" we may presume he has
in mind a wider audience of domestic slaves and workers
under the control of their *despotes,* "masters." There is
little doubt that the sense of freedom and dignity essential
to the gospel message must have created a deep tension in
the lives of Christians trapped in slavery. It is no accident
that several New Testament letters attempt to encourage
and comfort these Christians (cf., for example, 1 Cor 7:21-
24; Col 3:22-25; Eph 6:5-8). Although in 1 Corinthians Paul
tells the slaves to take advantage of any opportunity to gain
their freedom (an exception to his rule that everyone continue in the same position in which they received the gospel;

cf. above 2:13-17), neither he nor any New Testament writer offer a wholesale condemnation of slavery. The pervasiveness of the system and the risk to the community's existence that such a subversive program would entail seem to have prevented the early church from seeking such a radical insight. Only much later did the essential incompatibility between the *system* of slavery and the gospel become clear and urgent. But the roots of that liberation were already present in the christian message itself. And some signs of a new awareness can be found in the directives of the New Testament such as those of 1 Peter. The slaves are spoken to directly in the letter, without apology or condescension. They may be slaves within an economic system but not within the community. (Note the spirit of Paul's comment in 1 Cor 7:22, "For he who is called in the Lord as a slave is a freed man of the Lord."). Slaves are singled out only because the author realizes that they have a greater burden of suffering than anyone else.

The servants are to "be subject to" their masters. This advice fits neatly into the theology of 1 Peter. The servants, like all Christians (cf. 2:13), are to be fully active and responsible in the societal institutions to which they belong. This entails working with "kind and gentle" masters but also with the "overbearing" (the Greek word *skolios* used here has strong connotations, meaning "crooked" or "perverse"). But the author is not calling for a dehumanizing servility. Their "submission" is to be "with all respect." Our translation could lead the reader astray here. The word "respect" translates the Greek term *phobos*, "fear." The sense of the whole phrase is not that the servants are to obey their *masters* out of fear. "Fear" or reverence, as 2:17 makes clear (cf. also 1:17), is the awesome allegiance we owe *God*. Thus the phrase "with all respect" describes the religious consciousness of the slave as he or she goes about their duties. This is exactly what verses 19 and 20 state, although once again the translation we are using is somewhat inaccurate. The phrase "for one is approved" hardly does justice to the words of 1 Peter which literally say: "for this is a *grace (charis).*" The message is the same as the general principles stated above in 2:11-17. It is a "grace," God's gift of salvation, to be able to be mindful of God while having to suffer unjustly. The slave who has to suffer the conflict of working for a cruel or unjust master keeps his integrity and continues to do good by maintaining that inner freedom and integrity which spring from his relationship to God. The tenacious pursuit of good is at stake here (cf. v.20). Punishment that comes because of wrong deeds is without value. 1 Peter is not talking about any sort of masochistic fascination with sufferng. But when conflict and suffering are the result of doing good because of one's free loyalty to God, then this is a *grace* (the phrase "God's approval" at the end of verse 20 is another unsatisfying translation of the Greek which directly states: "this is a grace with God").

The plight of servants illustrates for the whole community what the vocation of a Christian involves. Because the experience of baptism has given us a new vision of life, we now see the world through God's eyes. The task is to build up a universe which will ultimately give glory to God. The creator's task and our work in the structures of society share the same goal and the same raw materials. Therefore the ability to pursue that good with integrity, even in situations of conflict and opposition, is a grace.

This broader lesson for all the Christians comes to the fore in verses 21-25. "For this you have been called . . ."; "this," namely the grace of pursuing God's good even at the price of suffering, is exactly what the Christian vocation in the world is all about. The Christians of Asia Minor had celebrated their "call" in baptism; now they are finding out what that call means. Their vocation to follow a way of creative suffering is a call to follow Jesus himself.

The power and example of the suffering Christ now consume the attention of the author. As we have already noted (cf. 1:11,19), 1 Peter refers to the passion of Jesus more than any other New Testament book. These verses (21-25) are one of three extended passages where the author probes this theme (cf. also 1:18-21; 3:18-22).

The sufferings of Christ have two levels of meaning for the Christian. His way of suffering was *"an example"* for us. He showed his disciples how one can suffer conflict, even death, and still "be mindful of God." But there is something more—his suffering is not only an example but itself has the *power* to bring about good. He suffered "for us." Both meanings of suffering apply to the Christians who have set out on their journey with Jesus; the endurance of pain not only can be a witness of courage and integrity but also can have a redemptive transforming power on behalf of others.

Both dimensions of suffering are reflected in the poetic words of verses 22-25. As in 1:18-21 much of the imagery is drawn from the Suffering Servant Song of Isaiah 53. The smooth cadence of these four verses suggests that the author may have borrowed them from an already existing Christian hymn. Verses 22-23 dwell on the example of the suffering Jesus; 24-25 speak of the redemptive power of his pain.

The words of verse 22 paraphrase Isaiah 53:9 ("... he had done no violence, and there was no deceit in his mouth"); Jesus like the slaves addressed in 18-20 was innocent. Verse 23 reshapes Isaiah 53:7 ("He was oppressed, and he was afflicted, yet he opened not his mouth..."); although suffering unjustly Jesus gave a good example. He did not allow his own goodness to be compromised by the hostility of his oppressors. The silence of Jesus the servant before the accusations of his captors is something that caught the attention of the gospel writers (cf. Mk 14:61; 15:5; Mk 26:63; 27:14; Lk 23:9; Jn 19:9-10). Matthew has Jesus explicitly reject the option of a violent response to his arrest (cf. Mt 26:52-54) thereby carrying out his own command in the Sermon on the Mount: "But I say to you, do not resist one who is evil. But if anyone strikes you on the right cheek, turn to him the other also" (Mt 5:39). Neither in the passion narratives nor in 1 Peter does the example of Jesus bespeak weakness. Only someone whose commitment to the gospel is

sound and disciplined can find the strength not to be so
overwhelmed by hostility that the values of the aggressor
suddenly displace one's own. This was the point in urging
slaves of an unjust master to act "with all reverence" for
God (v. 18) or to "be mindful of God." The same consciousness sustained the suffering Jesus who "entrusted himself
to the one who judges justly" (v. 23).

Verses 24-25 turn from the *example* of Jesus' sufferings
to their atoning *power*. Like the Servant of Israel who "bears
our iniquities" (Is 53:12), Jesus took on the burden of sin
in his passion. The crucifixion of Jesus is graphically stated:
"in his body on the tree." 1 Peter affirms a fundamental
belief of the christian tradition—Jesus, *the* human person,
the Son of God, in laying down his life out of fidelity to his
mission touches the life of every human being and enables
us to be free. His death is not simply an example of a gen-
erous martyrdom for others, but in God's mysterious providence it is an act of love which empowers others to live.
This salvific effect is reasserted in a series of images at the
conclusion of our passage. Jesus' death enables us to "die
to sin and live to righteousness" (v. 24). This phrase echoes
Paul's discussion of redemption in Romans 6 (e.g., "So you
also must consider yourselves dead to sin and alive to God in
Christ Jesus" (6:11). It also resonates with 1 Peter's repeated
references to the transformation which grace effects in a
christian's life (1:3; 1:14-15; 1:18-19; 1:22-23; 2:1-3; 2:9-10;
3:18,21; 4:1-2). Another image snatched from Isaiah 53:5—
"by his wounds you have been healed" — reasserts the
same idea.

The final verse (25) mines the Isaiah text again and speaks
of the pre-conversion plight of the Christian in pastoral
imagery—"for you were straying like sheep" (Is 53:6). But
now, through baptism, the wanderers have "turned back" to
the "shepherd and Guardian of your souls.". "Shepherd" as
an image for care and rescue has a long biblical pedigree.
The famed Psalm 23 speaks of Yahweh as the "Shepherd of
Israel." Ezekiel 34 contrasts the compassionate Shepherd
Yahweh with the unfaithful shepherds, the kings. Jesus'

parable of the lost sheep (Lk 15:3-7) draws on the same tradition to justify a ministry of compassion to tax collectors and sinners (cf. Lk 15:1-2). In Matthew 18:10-14 the same parable is now applied to the necessity of compassion for the weak members of the community. John's gospel propels the metaphor further by applying it to Jesus himself as the "Good Shepherd" (Jn 10:11). As a title for Jesus, Shepherd is also found in Hebrews 13:20 ("Jesus, the great Shepherd of the sheep") and in Apocalypse 7:17. The term "Guardian" reinforces the Shepherd's role as one of care and protection. The Greek word used here is *episcopos*, literally "overseer." In 5:1-4 Peter gives directives for those "elders" who have the responsibility of leadership in the community. He asks them to perform their role of "overseeing" *(episkopein)* after the example of the "Chief Shepherd" (5:4). Jesus, who gave his life for the ones he loves, is now the compassionate Guardian of these precious lives.

THE MISSION OF A CHRISTIAN WIFE.
3:1-6.

> 3 Likewise you wives, be submissive to your husbands, so that some, though they do not obey the word, may be won without a word by the behavior of their wives, ²when they see your reverent and chaste behavior. ³Let not yours be the outward adorning with braiding of hair, decoration of gold, and wearing of fine clothing, ⁴but let it be the hidden person of the heart with the imperishable jewel of a gentle and quiet spirit, which in God's sight is very precious. ⁵So once the holy women who hoped in God used to adorn themselves and were submissive to their husbands, ⁶as Sarah obeyed Abraham, calling him lord. And you are now her children if you do right and let nothing terrify you.

The plight of christian slaves, especially those in a diffii-cult conflict situation with unjust masters, had triggered a long reflection on the meaning of suffering (vv.18-25).

Now another difficult Christian role—a woman married to a non-christian husband—serves as a paradigm of christian mission for the entire community to consider. In the ancient world it was presumed that a woman would adopt the religious convictions of her husband. The same assumption is true in many patriarchal societies today. Although the author of 1 Peter shares some of his society's view of women, it is clear that the liberating force of the gospel has taken him far beyond what his contemporaries would dare think.

The basic principles of 1 Peter's "witness spirituality" (cf. 2:11-12) are applied to women as they were to servants— without apology or condescension. Even though women had a radically subordinate role in society, 1 Peter addresses them as free and equal in the christian community, indeed as having a demanding role that can serve as example for all the community. Therefore christian wives are to "be submissive to your husbands." The proper meaning of the word "submissive" needs to be re-emphasized (cf. comments above, under 2:13). The author is not trying to beat rebellious women back into line, nor is he calling for a second-class subordination of women. Wives are to be "submissive" in the sense that they are to continue to participate fully in the institution of marriage. Even though a "mixed marriage" (i.e., between a christian woman and a pagan husband) presents an extremely difficult challenge to the religious convictions of the wife, she is not to flee this situation but to continue in it.

As has been the case throughout this whole section of the letter (2:11-4:11), "participation in created institutions" is viewed as an opportunity to proclaim the gospel and to bring an unbelieving world to glorify its God (2:12). This mission need not be accomplished by direct religious persuasion. Instead 1 Peter has consistently called for the eloquent witness of a "good way of life" (2:12,15,20). This is how the christian citizen (2:13-17) or the christian servant (2:18-25) first preaches the gospel. The same advice is now offered to wives, especially those whose husbands "do not obey the word" (3:1). This phrase suggests that the author is referring to men who are not simply unbelievers, and therefore indifferent to christianity, but those who have *rejected* the gospel (cf. the comments under 2:8) and may well be hostile. This compounds the difficulties of the christian wife. Nevertheless, her response must be according to the pattern of the suffering Christ. It should be "without a word," implying that she does not return hostility for hostility (note 2:23: "when he was reviled he did not revile in return; when he suffered, he did not threaten"). Even more, her silent word is the eloquent gospel of a "beautiful way of life." The expression "way of life" (translated as "behavior" in verses 1 and 2) is the identical expression used in the key text of 2:12; it means a genuine christian life, one that "follows the steps" of Jesus (2:21). Two signs of that "way of life" are singled out. It is shot through with "reverence" or "fear"—that sense of awe and reverence for God that 1 Peter considers an essential part of christian holiness (cf. 1:17; 2:17; 2:18; the same Greek word "fear" is used in all of these texts, including 3:2 but is translated variously as "fear," "respect," "reverence"). And that way of life must be "chaste"; the wife even though caught in a difficult conflict is to be faithful to her marriage and her husband. This way of life—this silent word—can win over her husband. In 1 Peter the goal of every strategy is victory for God.

The author's reflections on the persuasiveness of a beautiful life continue in the next four verses, although the basic principles have already been stated. Verses 3-4 contrast the power of skin-deep beauty with that of the deep-down beauty of the heart. The text should not be construed as a puritanical attack on cosmetics or jewelry. The author's point is that in a human relationship, especially one of conflict in marriage, such superficial allurements soon fade. The marital track record of the "beautiful people" needs no comment. What does make a difference is the "hidden person of the heart." This quaint expression affirms that it is the values, the attitudes, the generosity of the human heart (all of these equivalent to the "hidden person") that

count in any lasting relationship. The author does not indulge in a bit of psychoanalysis here. By "hidden person"
he does not mean the unconscious or even the private
thoughts of a person. From the "hidden" (that is, not external) source of the "heart" (that is, the core of our human
person) comes the way of life that is the true measure of
human beauty. As is so often the case in 1 Peter, this imagery
seems to have its roots in the teaching imagery of Jesus
himself. Both Mark (7:1-23) and Matthew (15:1-20) re-
count Jesus' conflict with the Pharisees over the question
of ritual purity. The disciples' failure to eat with washed
hands (a violation of ritual law and not merely a failure of
hygiene for the Pharisees) draws fire from Jesus' enemies.
Jesus climaxes his rebuttal by stating that the only thing
which really defiles a human life is what comes from *within*—"for from within, out of the *heart* of a man" come
attitudes and behavior which are destructive.

This is the message of 1 Peter. That which beautifies
the christian wife and is likely to win over her husband is
not her dazzling accessories but "the imperishable jewel of
a gentle and quiet spirit" (v.5). "Gentleness" was considered
to be the archetypical virtue of women in Greek and Roman
society. Undoubtedly some of this cultural perspective has
influenced our author. In other words, he wants the woman
to be a genuinely good woman in the mode that his day
and age conceived of feminine goodness. But the christian
virtue of "gentleness" has much more bite than this. In
3:15 the author will call for *every* Christian—not just
women—to be "gentle." Gentleness is a quality that marks
the way Christians relate to other people out of respect
and compassion. In the majestic words of Matthew 11:29
Jesus describes himself as "gentle and lowly in heart" because he is open and inviting to those who are burdened.
"Gentleness" or "meekness" (the same Greek word *praus*
stands behind both adjectives) is the quality of those "who
inherit the earth" in the beatitude of Matthew 5:5. It is an
expression of strength not weakness because it is the quality
of those who are able to show love and compassion to others

even in the face of hostility. As such, it is "precious in God's eyes" (3:4).

An Old Testament example closes out 1 Peter's advice to wives. The great women of Israel who, like their christian descendants, "hoped in God" (cf. 1:21) used the same kind of precious "jewelry." They were faithful to God and were "submissive" to their husbands. The example of Sarah is singled out. Abraham was an important Old Testament figure for the early Christians (cf., for example, Rom 4). As the "Father of many nations" (the words of Gen 17:5 quoted by Paul in Rom 4:17) he was the one who had begun the great odyssey of God's people in which the Christians now participate. As one who is blessed by God because of his great faith (cf. Rom 4:3)—a faith that was exercised apart from the Jewish law—he was seen as the archetype of the Christians themselves. 1 Peter banks off this image of Abraham to speak of Sarah. Through baptism christian wives now step into the great company of God's people as they, like Sarah, "do right and let nothing terrify" them (3:6). The message is insistent. No human situation—not even the exceedingly demanding one which these women face—should immobilize their life of active witness. "Fear" in the sense of an unquestioned allegiance is owed to no situation or no person other than the Father of Jesus.

THE MISSION OF A CHRISTIAN HUSBAND.
3:7.

> [7]Likewise you husbands, live considerately with your wives, bestowing honor on the woman as the weaker sex, since you are joint heirs of the grace of life, in order that your prayers may not be hindered.

A quick reading of this verse might lead to the conclusion that the above-average marks 1 Peter gained in his attitude to women in the previous verses take a nose dive here. After telling servants and wives to be "submissive" that advice is *not* offered to the husbands. And women are labeled the "weaker sex." Although no amount of acrobatics could make the first century author of this letter a twentieth century feminist, we should be careful not to brand him an insensitive chauvinist either. This single verse bears responsible reading.

The inclusion of "husbands" in this part of the letter is probably due in great part to force of habit. The literary device of the "household list" (cf. above, 2:18) usually included major roles for husbands, wives, children or slaves, etc. But one senses that the interest of our author is not on the husband's situation; in the context of 1 Peter's major message (how to live out baptism in an alien world) the complex situations of servants and wives are much more instructive for the community, as we have already discussed. And even though not explicitly stated, the husbands are not exempt from "being submissive," anymore than the "all of you" in verse 8, the last category in the list. The basic principle, "be subject for the Lord's sake to every institution" (cf. 2:13), was directed to *every* Christian, man and woman. Therefore, a proper reading of 3:7 cannot allow the conclusion that wives are commanded "to be submissive" to their husbands while husbands are exempt. As we have noted at some length in discussing 2:13,18 and 3:1, the sense of the word "submissive" or "be subject to" (the same Greek word underlies both) means to *participate* and thus is not concerned primarily with an attitude of docility or subordination.

The designation of women as the "weaker sex," while obviously reflecting the attitude of a first century patriarchal society, is also surrounded by some qualifiers that make 1 Peter's description of the husband's role in marriage not as condescending to women as it might seem. Husbands are to live with their wives "considerately." This adverb is a translation of an intriguing Greek expression used by our author. Literally the text says "according to knowledge." "Considerately," therefore, does not mean "with kindness"—as the word might first strike us—but "with perception." Peter is asking the husbands to live with their wives in a way befitting the christian vision, with the "consciousness of God" that is the heritage of their baptism (cf. 2:19; 3:21). What this implies is brought out in the rest of the verse. The husband is to "honor" his wife and he is to do this even though society considers her the "weaker sex." An attitude of honor towards one that is deemed inferior is a result of the "knowledge" or "perception" that the gospel brings the husband. In the gospel vision women are not inferior or weaker at all but "joint heirs of the grace of life." That awesome inheritance has already been described in 1:4-5; it is the full experience of hope and salvation won for us by Jesus' death and resurrection. Paul's triumphant vision of salvation had led him to declare: "There is neither Jew nor Greek, there is neither slave nor free, there is neither male nor female, for you are all one in Christ Jesus" (Gal 3:21). For 1 Peter, as well, the eschatological vision of a world ultimately graced by God must even now flood the perception and change the attitudes of us who live in a time when society still holds some unfree.

The advice to husbands to honor and reverence their wives is given one more motivation. A good relationship between husband and wife will prevent their prayers from being "hindered." The conviction that the quality of one's prayer is tied to the quality of one's human relationships goes far back into biblical tradition. The prophets scourged the conscience of Israel for the cleavage between its liturgical life and its social life. Worship that papered over wholesale injustice was worthless tissue and nothing more (cf. Is 1:10-17). Jesus, too, has warned against attempting prayer without working at reconciliation: "So if you are offering your gift at the altar, and there remember that your brother has something against you, leave your gift there before the altar and go; first be reconciled to your brother, and then come and offer your gift" (Mt 5:23-24). Indeed, the link between love of God and love of neighbor stands at the epicenter of Jesus' message. What is true for the community in general (cf. the next section 3:8-12) is surely true for the

primary structure in christian community, the family. Therefore, the honor offered to God in the couples' prayer will be
flawed if the honor they bestow on each other has dimmed.

THE MISSION OF EVERY CHRISTIAN: TO BLESS. 3:8-12.

> [8]Finally, all of you, have unity of spirit, sympathy, love
> of the brethren, a tender heart and a humble mind. [9]Do
> not return evil for evil or reviling for reviling; but on the
> contrary bless, for to this you have been called, that you
> may obtain a blessing. [10]For
> "He that would love life
> and see good days,
> let him keep his tongue from evil
> and his lips from speaking guile;
> [11]let him turn away from evil and
>   do right;
> let him seek peace and pursue it.
> [12] For the eyes of the Lord are upon
>   the righteous,
> and his ears are open to their prayer.
> But the face of the Lord is against
>   those that do evil."

The list of people who are the beneficiaries of Peter's
special advice comes to a close. Now he addresses everyone,
calling for that which is basic to all christian witness: the
mutual love and respect which binds Christians together.
This same message anchored his exhortations in chapter 1
(cf. 1:22) and will do so again in chapter 4 (cf. 4:8-11) and
chapter 5 (5:5).

He names five qualities that characterize a vibrant christian community. All are to have "unity of spirit." This phrase
captures well the connotation of the Greek word *homo-
phrones*, or "like-mindedness," which does not imply pro-
grammed thinking but a kinship of spirit that allows diver-
gent views in an atmosphere of mutual respect. Paul pleads

for the same virtue in Philippians 2:2-6. A second quality is that of mutual "sympathy"; as the word states, to "feel with" each other and thereby become compassionate for the burdens and supportive of the dreams that belong to someone else (cf. Paul's words in Rom 12:15, "rejoice with those who rejoice, weep with those who weep. . .") The qualities of "like-mindedness" and "sympathy" lead to a third, "love," love rooted in "a tender heart" and "a humble mind." "Tender-heartedness," literally, "good feeling towards" another, is a quality spoken of in the New Testament to characterize an attitude of compassion for others. The sight of his lost son coming back home kindles the "feeling" of compassion in the father in Jesus' story of the Prodigal Son (Lk 15:20). The king is "moved with pity" toward the errant servant in Matthew 18:20 and it is "feeling" that halts the Samaritan alongside the robber's victim in Luke 10:33. Paul loves his Philippian Christians with the very "feeling" that Jesus had for them (Phil 1:8). This rush of compassion is what we owe each other, 1 Peter states. And along with a sense of compassion is a need for the quality of "humble-mindedness." Unless a person is capable of transcending his or her own needs and able to look at others with reverence, no real community life can endure.

In addition to these qualities one crucial attitude is emphasized: rather than "return evil for evil or reviling for reviling" the very nature of a christian vocation urges them to react with a "blessing" (v.9). One can surmise that 1 Peter intends this advice not only for the internal life of the community but for its relationships to non-community members as well. The emphasis on this christian virtue is characteristic of 1 Peter's entire view of christian existence. The cycle of violence—of hostility for hostility—must be broken because it is "unreal." Christian experience shows that "reality," God's reality, has another pattern. Despite the bankruptcy of their lives, God does not repay the human family with a curse or condemnation but with infinite mercy, blessing (cf. 2:10 and repeatedly through the first three chapters). The Christians were called to a blessing not to destruction. Jesus himself had set the pattern of a human existence according to God's truth, "when he was reviled, he did not revile in return" (2:23). Slaves and wives, who know what revilement meant, were asked to follow the same pattern (cf. 2:18-25; 3:1-6). To bring a blessing to the world, to provoke it to glorify God by the witness of good living, is the christian mission.

A sizeable quote from Psalm 34:13-17 is worked into the letter (vv.10-12) to confirm the author's exhortation. The theme of "doing good" has run throughout the entire section that began in 2:11. The message of the psalm ratifies this theme: the relentless pursuit of good, even in the face of hostility, can lead one to life and to God. The choice of evil brings death.

THE BLESSED TESTIMONY OF HOPE.
3:13-17.

> [13]Now who is there to harm you if you are zealous for what is right? [14]But even if you do suffer for righteousness' sake, you will be blessed. Have no fear of them, nor be troubled, [15]but in your hearts reverence Christ as Lord. Always be prepared to make a defense to any one who calls you to account for the hope that is in you, yet do it with gentleness and reverence; [16]and keep your conscience clear, so that, when you are abused, those who revile your good behavior in Christ may be put to shame. [17]For it is better to suffer for doing right, if that should be God's will, than for doing wrong.

All throughout this exhortation section of the epistle (2:11-4:11) the author has presumed that discipleship exacts a cost. For many, such as servants and wives, it may bring open abuse. For all, it means the disciplined love needed for community living and the constant effort to witness to a life of integrity. This cost of discipleship now becomes the dominant concern in the latter half of the exhortation section (3:13-4:11).

The quotations from Psalm 34 which concluded the previous section (cf. vv.10-12) had summed up 1 Peter's exhortations in the basic contrast between "doing right" and "doing evil." The pursuit of good in the face of evil is where this new paragraph picks up the thread of the epistle: "Now who is there to harm you if you are zealous for what is right?" (v.13). The question rings with 1 Peter's unshakable optimism. It is obvious from the entire epistle that "harm" in many forms has already touched the Christians: they are "in exile," they are ridiculed and abused (4:4), and worse than abuse seems to lurk in the future. Harm has come, but the "harm" 1 Peter speaks of here is of a different order. No *real* harm, no ultimate threat, can penetrate the love and hope which is God's gift to the Christian. The thought is reminiscent of what may be the most soaring passage in all of Pauline literature: "Who shall separate us from the love of Christ? . . . For I am sure that neither death, nor life, nor angels, nor principalities, nor things present, nor things to come, nor powers, nor height, nor depth, nor anything else in all creation, will be able to separate us from the love of God in Christ Jesus our Lord" (Rom 8:35,38-39).

1 Peter moves his thought another notch. Not only is the one who pursues the good protected from ultimate harm, he or she is "blessed" because their suffering is for the sake of righteousness. The words seem to paraphrase one of Jesus' beatitudes in Matthew 5:10: "Blessed are those who are persecuted for righteousness' sake for theirs is the kingdom of heaven. The sufferings spoken of are a direct conse- quence of the christian's perseverance in doing good; there- fore, they participate in God's redemptive struggle to mold the world into beauty (cf. above 2:13,21-25). This is a blessing!

The author wants to soothe the anxieties of his Christians as they read the storm signals on the horizon (the word "suffering" in v.14 is in the optative mood in Greek, "you might suffer"—suggesting that the worst was still yet to come; cf. also v.17). A snatch of Isaiah 8:12 serves his pur- pose: "Have no fear of what they fear, nor be troubled"

(the RSV's translation "Have no fear of them" is a trunca-
tion of what 1 Peter's words actually say). The original text
of Isaiah goes on to say: "But the Lord of hosts, him you
shall regard as holy; let him be your fear, and let him be your
dread" (Is 8:13). There is little doubt that this unquoted
statement of Isaiah is on Peter's mind as he writes: "but in
your hearts reverence Christ as *Lord.*" *Kyrios* or "Lord"
is one of the most exalted titles applied to Jesus in the New
Testament. As the Isaiah text illustrates it was a title used
of Yahweh in the Old Testament. In the New Testament it
was applied to Jesus to underscore his authority as the
Risen Christ to whom the Christians owed allegiance and
reverence. That is the mood here. No Christian need be
terrorized or made a prisoner of the slavish fears that human
powers attempt to wield over people (cf. comments under
2:16-17; 1:17). Christian "fear" is of an entirely different
nature—it is the loving awe one owes to God himself (2:17);
it is touched by the reverence (the word used in v. 15 literally
means to "treat as holy") and loyalty owed to Christ as our
Lord. It is from the "heart," a loving commitment of the
total person.

1 Peter is not calling for some kind of christian macho,
with fearless Jesus people coolly facing down the agents of
evil. The author never forgets the goal of the christian
mission and he never loses sight of the pattern of Jesus'
own sufferings. The ultimate purpose of doing right in spite
of adversity is not to beat the competition but to serve it.
This compassionate sense of mission breaks out in what
may be the most frequently quoted verse of the epistle:
"Always be prepared to make a defense to any one who calls
you to account for the hope that is in you; yet do it with
gentleness and reverence" (3:15). Practically every word
in the verse is a distillation of 1 Peter's central message.

"Hope" seems to be a code word in 1 Peter for the whole
attitude a Christian should have toward life. It is equivalent
to what Paul calls "faith"; a radical trust in God that shapes
our very lives. The author has spoken explicitly of this hope
throughout the letter. God's mercy is the starting point for

hope (1:3), and his faithful promise to fulfill our dreams makes hope the expectation of our future (1:13,21). This sense of hope is what ultimately separates a Christian from a non-believer. And the author is convinced that a genuine christian life ("doing good," as he repeatedly calls it) will become a provocative question mark for those who live with little meaning: "With things the way they are why do you have hope?" The answer to that question—"a defense of hope"—is what the christian mission in the world is all about. The "defense" (literally, an "apology" for hope or speaking on hope's behalf) is made not only by the example of one's life but by an intelligent explanation of the reasons for it to any one who asks. The presumption here is that christianity is not only an experience or a style of life but that it has a rationale which has been reflected on and can be communicated to someone else. This, in fact, is what the author of the letter has been doing for the Christians themselves; reviewing the origins of their faith, putting it into historical perspective, and pointing out the values that fit a christian world view. That is a mission every mature Christian should be ready to do when the situation calls for it. Apologetics, in other words, is part of the christian mission.

But the exercise of this responsibility must not betray its goal or the gospel it intends to proclaim. The "style" one uses in defending hope must be imbued with the same values that are intrinsic to a life of hope. Here again the whole spirit of the letter is in evidence. The response to a non-believer's challenge should be "with gentleness," the compassionate concern and respect that typifies the way a Christian relates to every human being as a creation of God (cf. above, 3:4). And it should be in a spirit of "reverence." The word used here is, literally, "fear," the same word that 1 Peter has consistently used to describe one's relationship to *God* (cf. 1:17; 2:17,18; 3:2). Thus "reverence" or "fear" is not the attitude to be taken toward the pagan questioner—which would contradict the advice in the previous verse ("have no fear of them")—but towards God. In other words, in dealing gently with the questioner one should also be bolstered by a sense of reverence and awe for God. Looking at the whole situation with the eyes of faith is what enables the Christians to have hope in the first place and that same vantage point pushes them to proclaim it with sensitivity to others.

The atmosphere of this passage and of the letter as a whole suggests that the kind of encounter between Christian and non-Christians envisaged here is not a friendly conversation over coffee. Words like "harm" and "suffering," and the encouragement to have no "fear," "to be gentle" show that the pagans are angrily challenging the Christians' hope because it threatens them and throws them off balance. This is clearly the implication of the message in verses 16 and 17 which continue the discussion of the "style" needed for a christian defense of hope. Their "conscience must be clear." In 1 Peter as well as in Paul "conscience" means more than just the faculty that prompts us to good and indicts us for evil. As the etymology of the word suggests, it has to do with knowledge, with a *consciousness* that is both the source and quality control for action. In 1 Peter 2:19 the servants were urged to endure pain by "being mindful of God." That phrase translates the same Greek root used here for "conscience" in 3:16. In 3:21 the word appears again, describing baptism as "an appeal to God for a clear conscience." In all of these texts *consciousness* helps add the right dimension to what we mean by conscience. The Christians' consciousness of God is what gives backbone to their "conscience"; awareness of God leads to right judgement and right action. That integrity will be necessary in order to withstand the abuse that may be a consequence of fidelity to the gospel. "Good behavior in Christ" could lead to something more than grudging admiration or idle curiosity. Sometimes a good life is a searing prophetic challenge to the way other people live and they can react with "abuse." Only a life thoroughly rooted "in Christ" is likely to withstand the pressure to conform. The phrase "in Christ" is a patent expression of Paul's theology, summarizing the believer's life bond with Christ. 1 Peter is the only other New Testament author to use this phrase (cf. also 5:10,14). It has some of the same flavor as in Paul's writings, but seems to typify a pattern of behavior rather than the mystical bond of faith and love.

The passage concludes (v. 17) with a message that has been heard before in this letter. Suffering abuse in itself has nothing to recommend it. If that abuse is caused by wrong behavior on the Christians' part, they can take no pride in that. Only when abuse is part of the cost of genuine discipleship does it become salvific. If God should will that the Christians walk this path, then they are blessed because they are sharing in God's own creative struggle to bring the world to glory.

THE FRONTIERS OF GOD'S SALVATION.
3:18-22.

> [18]For Christ also died for sins once for all, the righteous for the unrighteous, that he might bring us to God, being put to death in the flesh but made alive in the spirit; [19]in which he went and preached to the spirits in prison, [20]who formerly did not obey, when God's patience waited in the days of Noah, during the building of the ark, in which a few, that is, eight persons, were saved through water. [21]Baptism, which corresponds to this, now saves you, not as a removal of dirt from the body but as an appeal to God for a clear conscience, through the resurrection of Jesus Christ, [22]who has gone into heaven and is at the right hand of God, with angels, authorities, and powers subject to him.

The previous call to be gentle and to offer a fearless witness of hope (3:13-17) finds its basis in Jesus' death for us. As he has done twice before in his letter, the author binds a plea for christian witness with a penetrating reflection on the passion of Christ (cf. 1:18-21; 2:22-25). The style of this passion meditation, especially verse 18, is similar to the other two; the language is so rich and so condensed that many scholars conclude the author borrowed some of this material from an already existing hymn or creed that summarized the reflections of the early Christians. As we will see, a number of "code words" and images are used here to describe the effects of Jesus' death and resurrection.

The point of this christological passage is not simply to bring the example of Jesus before the eyes of the Christians but to plot the *range* of his saving acts. His "testimony of hope" touched not only the Christians through their baptism but broke the cosmic boundaries, rescuing the "spirits in prison" and striking awe and obedience in the heavenly powers. By surveying this wide frontier of God's salvation, the author wants to bolster the resolve of his Christians to continue their own witness even in the face of suffering.

The opening verse (v. 18) replays the theme of the previous section, but now roots it in the example of Jesus. It is valuable when christian suffering brings life to others; that, after all, is what Jesus has done for us. Jesus' death "brought us to God." Because of variations in the ancient manuscripts, it is difficult to determine the precise wording of this verse. Some manuscripts have "suffered for" rather than "died for" and include the phrase "for us" or "for you" after the phrase "for sins." None of these variants change the basic meaning of the text, however.

Each successive phrase in the verse emphatically states that the suffering and death of Jesus saved us. The first affirms that Christ died "for sins." The word "for" has a sense of purpose (not result). To do something about the plight of humanity trapped in sin was the goal of Jesus' entire mission, a mission which climaxed on the cross. Next the author notes that it was a definitive act: "once for all." Through Jesus' self-giving God defeated sin; it has no more radical power over human destiny. Paul uses the same phrase—"once for all"—with the same basic meaning in

Romans 6:10. The next phrase repeats the message but now with the language of "justice": he died as "the righteous for the unrighteous." In 3:14, a verse that reflects the beautitude of Matthew 5:10, those who suffered on behalf of "righteousness" or "justice" were declared blessed. "Justice" is a strong biblical concept. God himself is "just" because he is faithful to his promises. *Human* justice means, in turn, a faithful response to God. The "just" ones of the Old Testament were those Israelites who remained obedient to God's law. In previous reflections on the suffering of Jesus, our author used the language and imagery of the Suffering Servant Song found in Isaiah 53. That seems to be the case here. The Servant is called the "righteous one" and his fidelity in suffering "make(s) many to be accounted righteous" (Is 53:11). Jesus, the just man, gives his life for the sake of those who are unfaithful (cf. the same thought in 2:24). Another redemptive image flashes on the screen with the words "that he might bring us to God." "Journey" has been a leitmotif in much of 1 Peter's description of christian life (cf., for example, 1:13; 2:21). Here the whole saga of redemption is pictured as a struggle to reach God, an image found in a number of New Testament writings (especially Hebrews; cf. Heb 10:19-22; 12:22-23; also Eph 2:18; 3:12). Jesus, like a sure guide, leads us into God's presence.

All of these redemptive images rest on the death and resurrection of Jesus. 1 Peter underscores this fact with the words, "being put to death in the flesh but made alive in the spirit." The "flesh-spirit" antithesis, used often in the New Testament, calls for careful interpretation. As we noted above in discussing 2:11, "flesh" does not usually mean the "body" as opposed to the "soul," or the "material" as opposed to the "spiritual." Rather the terms "flesh" and "spirit" each refer to the totality of the human person viewed from different vantage points. "Flesh" describes humanity as related to God and therefore free, living, transcendent. In verse 18, then, 1 Peter is *not* saying Jesus' body (his "flesh") died but his soul ("spirit") is alive. Rather, he is saying that

Jesus himself experienced the redemptive process: he was "put to death in the flesh," that is, he suffered the limitations of the human condition but through the power of God's grace he transcended them. He was "made alive to the spirit": that is, because of Jesus' fidelity and his trust in the Father, he was raised to new life. Describing the experience of christian life as a movement from "flesh to spirit" is frequent in Paul (cf., for example, Rom 8:3-13). What is intriguing about these words in 1 Peter is that they apply to *Jesus* himself—he walks with us in the struggle to reach God.

Jesus' work of salvation now moves beyond the range of our own experience into the murky underworld (vv.19-20). This is one of the most unusual passages in the entire letter, and, indeed, a rare statement in the New Testament as a whole. To understand what the author might mean we have to recall the biblical cosmic map. For many centuries, the Jews had no clear idea of life after death. At best the dead endured some shadowy existence in Sheol, the dim underworld. But this was hardly existence at all since the dead were cut off from God, the only source of life (cf. Ps 115:17: "The dead do not praise the Lord, nor do any that go down into silence."). However, under the impact of Greek and Persian thought, and stimulated by their own persistent belief in God's mercy, the Jews developed a firmer belief in life beyond death. Eventually words like "immortality" and "resurrection" became part of biblical vocabulary (cf. Wis 3:4, Dan 12:2). The dead, at least those who had been faithful to God during their lifetime, awaited the final age when Yahweh's life-giving power would spring them from the prison of Sheol. This seems to be the scenario for our passage.

1 Peter uses this tradition and the cosmology it implies to add another zone to Jesus' saving work. "Alive in the spirit" Jesus goes and preaches to the dead in the prison of Sheol. He is a herald of the gospel even here, where the effects of sin are so dramatically evident. The author has in mind a particular group of the dead. These shadow human beings

are not the faithful saints of the Old Testament whose eventual salvation was expected by later Jewish tradition (there is reference to them in Mt 27:52-53) but people who had sinned—the vast throngs of humanity who had spurned God's call to repentance in the days of Noah and who were subsequently destroyed in the flood. The hope-filled missionary stance of 1 Peter is quaintly expressed here. The flood had an important symbolic meaning in biblical tradition. It dramatized the whole story of salvation: humanity's failure, the ultimate moment of judgement, God's promise of rescue in spite of sin. God had attempted to bring humanity to its senses—his "patience had waited" while the warning sign of the building of the ark might take effect. But wickedness blinded people to the warning and only eight just people were rescued from the water (cf. the story in Gen 7:13). But God's plan to save humanity would not be thwarted even by human malice. The disobedient souls who had perished in the flood have a second chance; Jesus himself—the missionary of hope par excellence—breaks into their prison of death and brings them God's good news of rescue.

The reason for 1 Peter's choice of the Noah story may be found in verse 21. The Christian's experience of rescue from the "prison of death" took place in water, too! Not the waters of a flood but the gentle waters of baptism. The seascape is vastly different but the effects are the same: "Baptism now saves you!" The word "now" suggests to some interpreters of 1 Peter that the baptismal ceremony would be taking place at this very moment, and therefore the original form of the letter may have been a homily addressed to baptismal candidates. But this is unlikely. The overall message of 1 Peter is not about baptism as such but about the living out of the christian vocation received at baptism. The "now" is not a time reference to the ritual act of baptism but points to another category in a succession of salvation experiences. Noah and his family experienced it at the time of the flood. The dead who languished in Sheol experienced it when Christ brought them the message of rescue. And "now" we, this generation, experienced it too at baptism.

Thus the "now" checks off another point in the wide range of God's saving action.

The experience of salvation in baptism is described as a new "consciousness," an image 1 Peter favors and one that is unique in the entire New Testament (cf. 3:16 and 2:19). Even though water is involved, the effect of baptism is not a mere washing away of dirt from a body; its cleansing effect penetrates into the very center of our being, into "the hidden person of the heart" as the author put it in 3:4. Baptism is "an appeal to God for a clear conscience." Through this act the sinners, as it were, ask God to transform their lives so that they can see the world with the clear eye of faith and have the strength to act in accordance with the beautiful vision of creation God gives. Even though the author describes baptism as "appeal" there is no doubt that the appeal is heard by God, because this appeal, the longing for a new consciousness, is "through the resurrection of Jesus." In 1:3 the author had described baptism as a new birth in hope "through the resurrection of Jesus Christ from the dead." Now that great saving act of Jesus is cited again as the source of our Christian existence; this time not with new birth imagery but with the image of a new perception of reality. Conscience or "consciousness" imagery is apt here because the whole point of this passage is to spur the Christian to courageous good works.

A final sweep on the horizon of salvation takes place in verse 22. The Jesus who saves us in baptism and who takes his work of salvation into the hopeless underworld is the same one who by his resurrection is exalted "at the right hand of God." This image of triumph is taken from Psalm 110:1, a coronation hymn that described the anointing of the king by God as an enthronement "at my right hand." This psalm is frequently cited in the New Testament to proclaim Jesus' exaltation by the Father (cf. Mk 12:36; Acts 2:33,34; Eph 1:20; Col 3:1; Heb 1:13). This exaltation is the final chapter in Jesus' redemptive struggle; he reaches the goal of his journey to God (cf. 3:18) and at that moment of triumphant homecoming he subjugates the cosmic powers. This cosmic rule of the risen Jesus is affirmed in many passages of the New Testament, as in the powerful opening chapter of Ephesians (1:20-23) or in Paul's preview of the final triumph of Jesus in 1 Corinthians (15:24-28). The ancient world speculated that the universe was populated with spirits and powers, some of which controlled the stars and had a hand in human destiny. How much of this world view was endorsed by the early Christians is not always clear. But of one thing they were sure: whatever spirits or powers might lurk in the universe, they were subordinate to the victorious Christ. This is the meaning of Paul's ardent text in Romans 8:38-39 where he takes an inventory of the possible forces of the cosmos and confidently concludes that nothing can separate him from "the love of God in Christ Jesus our Lord." That same conviction is affirmed by 1 Peter 3:22—the "angels, authorities and powers" are subject to the risen Lord.

This whole passage has taken us over a trajectory of salvation; from the death and resurrection of Jesus (v.18) to his descent into Sheol (v.19) to his triumphant exaltation at God's right hand (v.22). Although this "journey" imagery (specifically the descent into Sheol) is unique in the New Testament, it is a theme picked up in the writings of the early Fathers and used in the creed. For 1 Peter, too, this saving journey was part of the "creed" on which the energetic witness of the community must be based.

LIVING IN THE SPIRIT.
4:1-6.

4 Since therefore Christ suffered in the flesh, arm yourselves with the same thought, for whoever has suffered in the flesh has ceased from sin, ²so as to live for the rest of the time in the flesh no longer by human passions but by the will of God. ³Let the time that is past suffice for doing what the Gentiles like to do, living in licentiousness, passions, drunkenness, revels, carousing, and lawless idolatry. ⁴They are surprised that you do not now

> join them in the same wild profligacy, and they abuse you;
> 5but they will give account to him who is ready to judge
> the living and the dead. 6For this is why the gospel was
> preached even to the dead, that though judged in the flesh
> like men, they might live in the spirit like God.

We have described the basic message of 1 Peter as a "witness spirituality." Two principles undergird his conception of christian life: a call for inner freedom and the commission to give a living witness of hope (cf. 2:11-12). In the sections of the epistle we have just completed (the "lists" of 2:18-3:12, the general exhortations of 3:13-17 and the christological reflection in 3:18-22) the main concern of the author was the mission of witness. Living a good life and even having to suffer for it can bring about the salvation of the world, just as Christ's own sufferings have done. Now the author turns to his other principle, the need for inner freedom.

Once again Jesus' sufferings are invoked but this time not as a pattern of witness but of conversion. Jesus' "suffering in the flesh," that is the suffering involved in giving himself for others, entailed a purification, a self-transcendence which is the very opposite of sin (cf. 3:18). The Christians are told to "arm themselves" with the same perception. This military imagery is also found in Paul (cf. 1 Thess 5:8; 2 Cor 6:7; Rom 13:12-14 and especially in Eph 6:11-17) and connotes a sense of disciplined readiness for mission.

Inner freedom is achieved by breaking away from slavery to "human passions." As we noted in discussing 2:11 living free of "human passion" is not a call for cold-blooded rigorism. By "passion" the author means those self-destructive tendencies that all of us experience, those which are the very opposite of the "will of God" (v.2). Whenever 1 Peter broaches this topic he seems to be aware of the history of his young Christian community. They knew what he meant by the kind of passion that could snuff out meaning and joy in a human life; they had been adrift in that world of despair themselves. So here (vv.2-4) he looks at history from a christian perspective. The *"time is past"* for living

a life of slavery (literally, "for the desires of the pagans")—
that was a time of despair and the author cites a standard
list of its symptoms (as in 2:1). It was a time of "lawless
idolatry," a label for pagan religions used frequently by
Jews and the early Christians (cf. for example, Rom 1:18;
1 Thess 1:9; Gal 4:8-11). They were, in other words, living a
life out of touch with God. But *now*, through baptism, they
have crossed into a completely new time zone; now they look
forward to *the rest of time* (v.2), to the glorious fulfillment
of creation when all the world will be suffused with the glory
of God (cf. 2:12). As noted before, the author believes that
this period of history will quickly run its course (cf. 1:6; 4:7).

This shift in the christian's view of history is parallelled
by a transformation in their lives, a transformation that may
cause surprise and even hostility among their pagan neighbors (v.4). A more literal translation of this verse helps
bring out its forceful meaning: "they are shocked you do not
go along with them into the same flood of despair (literally
"non-salvation") and they blaspheme you." The pagan
world was a journey into hopelessness; the Christians had
found the way to life. Their refusal to conform kindled abuse
from the pagans. Literally, 1 Peter calls it "blasphemy"
because in attacking the Christians the pagans were unwit-
tingly attacking God's own people, his "living temple" (cf.
2:4-10). Although the mood of 1 Peter is consistently upbeat
he does not shy away from the hard consequences of human
choice (cf. 1:17; 2:8; 4:17). To mock the gospel, to abuse the
Christian, is something for which the hostile pagans are
accountable to God. It is significant that the author explicitly leaves the task of judgement to God—not to the
Christians. As 1 Peter repeatedly urges, the Christian
response to abuse is not more abuse but blessing (cf. 3:9).

The missionary stance of the letter cannot be quelled for
long. The final verse of this segment seems to sum up what
has gone before. "For this"—the transformation from a
history of despair to a future of hope (4:1-5), the strength
to do good for others even at the cost of suffering (3:13-22)—
was the purpose of Jesus' own mission, a message of hope

that took him "even to the dead." The range and power of God's salvation sweeps far beyond our expectation (cf. the message of 3:18-22). Thus God's "judgement"—his ultimate call to life and the opportunity for human response—was brought by Christ to the dead. Now it comes to the *living* dead, those trapped in a life of despair, through the gospel witness of the Christians. The goal of all this is that those who are "in the flesh" (limited, enslaved, hopeless) might "live in the spirit" (free, loving, hope-filled). To live this way is to live "like God" (v.6).

LIFE WITHIN A COMMUNITY OF WITNESS. 4:7-11.

> [7]The end of all things is at hand; therefore keep sane and sober for your prayers. [8]Above all hold unfailing your love for one another, since love covers a multitude of sins. [9]Practice hospitality ungrudgingly to one another. [10]As each has received a gift, employ it for one another, as good stewards of God's varied grace: [11]whoever speaks, as one who utters oracles of God; whoever renders service, as one who renders it by the strength which God supplies; in order that in everything God may be glorified through Jesus Christ. To him belong glory and dominion for ever and ever. Amen.

In the previous paragraph the author had spelled out the necessity of inner freedom for those who wait and work for the final day of salvation. Now his instructions turn to the *communal* dimension of christian living. The tone of the community's life should reflect its consciousness that it moves toward the fulfillment of history.

The segment begins with a strong assertion about the future: "the end of all things is at hand" (v.7). The language is typical of New Testament terminology for the end of the world, the moment of the Lord's glorious return and completion of the work of salvation. Earlier in the letter 1 Peter had indicated his belief that this glorious moment was not far off (cf. 1:6). This was a dominant note in the previous section (4:1-6); the time of slavery to passion is over; the time for "life in the spirit" is here. Whenever the New Testament speaks of the "end of the world" it is not concerned merely with a cosmic timetable but with a *quality of life* based on a conviction about reality. If we are destined for life with God, if our future is one of hope not despair, then this should make a difference in our lives *now*. Conversion is not meant to be an act of desperation before the dam breaks, but a measured response to the *truth* about ourselves and our world.

This is the spirit of 1 Peter in this section. The approach of the endtime leads to a "therefore," a plea that the community's life would be appropriate to its sense of destiny and its mission in the world. The Christian should be "sane" and "sober"—a brace of virtues frequently coupled with discussions of the endtime in the New Testament (in 1 Peter 1:13; 5:8; cf. also 1 Thess 5:1-10; Mk 13:33-37 and parallels). Reflection on the end should not cause hysteria about when and how the end will come about. Instead the nearness of the end should heighten the community's awareness of God's loving presence. Panic or undue emotion would disrupt the community and impede one's readiness to pray (cf. a similar concern in 3:7).

The community should be alert to live as God's people. Therefore the paramount concern must be their "love for one another." As we have noted before, the call for mutual love is always the bottom line in 1 Peter's instructions to the community (cf. the discussion under 1:22). Such persevering love "covers a multitude of sins." This often quoted phrase is found in Proverbs 10:12 and is repeated in James 5:20 as well as in the Letters of Clement, two early patristic writings. The meaning seems captured in the original quote from Proverbs: "Hatred stirs up strife, but love covers all offenses." Persistent love can soothe the tension and heal the wounds that are an inevitable part of any community living.

That first principle—"unfailing love for one another"—is now concretized through a number of gifts and services. The Christians should "practice hospitality ungrudgingly" (v.9). This was an important virtue in the early church. Many small, tightly knit communities flung across the Roman empire needed to maintain communication with each other if they were to remain God's *people*. The gospel literature encourages hospitality to the missionaries who wandered from place to place (cf. Mt 10:11-15; 40-42). And the practice of having the local community gather for worship in private homes would also necessitate hospitality (Paul refers to house churches, cf. for example, 1 Cor 16:19; Rom 16:5; Col 4:15). This hospitality should be offered "ungrudgingly": communication and generosity were no less difficult for the earliest Christians than they are now.

The author now considers community "gifts" or "charism"; these, too, must be employed in a spirit of mutual love. In 1 Corinthians 14 and Romans 12 Paul discussed the "charisms" or the special gifts given by the Spirit to be used for the benefit of the community. 1 Peter seems to work out of a similar but not identical tradition. For 1 Peter the source of the gifts is God's "varied grace." Each Christian is endowed with these various gifts and they must be used for "service" on behalf of the community. (The author uses the word *diakonein* in verse 10, a quasi-technical form for service in the New Testament.) This will make the Christians "good stewards," an image used in some of Jesus' own parables which call for responsibility while awaiting the end time (cf. Mt 24:45-51; 25:14-30; Lk 12:42-48). The author does not list specific charisms as Paul does but concentrates on the spirit in which they are to be used. "Whoever speaks" is to do so "as one who utters oracles of God" (v.11). God's word brings life (cf. 1:23-25) and that is what the loving words of the Christian should do. "Whoever serves" should do it "by the strength which God supplies." God's power is a creative force moving the world to salvation. This way of speaking and acting defines what "God consciousness"—the effect of baptism (cf. 2:19; 3:21)—means.

The goal of living in community this way is "that in everything God may be glorified through Jesus Christ." 1 Peter's great vision of a world ready to break out in worship of its loving God is summoned up again (cf. 2:12). Throughout his long list of instructions, beginning in 2:11, the author has had his eye fixed on this vision of glory. All of Jesus' life, all of his suffering witness on behalf of others, was directed to God. So, too, every act of the Christian—the suffering of slaves and wives, the struggle for inner freedom, the effort to build a community of love—all of this must be directed to God's glory. That dream triggers a prayer of praise: "to him"—that is, the Father of Jesus—"belong glory and dominion for ever and ever. Amen."

Part III.
Final Instructions to a Suffering Church.
4:12–5:14.

The third and final section of the epistle now begins. An acclamation of praise brought the previous section to a halt with verse 11. The address "beloved" in verse 12 indicates the author's awareness that he is moving toward his finish (the same word had inaugurated the second major section in 2:11). The finality of the doxology in 4:11 and the more urgent tone of the exhortations in this last section have led some commentators to speculate that this new section was originally independent of 2:11–4:11. But the dynamic of bringing his message to a close seems a more likely solution to the difference in tone. Few new themes are introduced. Points already discussed in the letter are marshalled together as the author recalls the necessity and the value of suffering (4:12-19) and appeals for good leadership (5:1-5) and persevering discipleship (5:6-11). Some brief words of greeting close the letter (5:12-14).

SUFFERING AS A CHRISTIAN.
4:12-19.

> [12]Beloved, do not be surprised at the fiery ordeal which comes upon you to prove you, as though something strange were happening to you. [13]But rejoice in so far as you share Christ's sufferings, that you may also rejoice and be glad when his glory is revealed. [14]If you are reproached for the name of Christ, you are blessed, because the spirit of glory and of God rests upon you. [15]But let

none of you suffer as a murderer, or a thief, or a wrong-doer, or a mischief-maker; [16]yet if one suffers as a Christian, let him not be ashamed, but under that name let him glorify God. [17]For the time has come for judgement to begin with the household of God; and if it begins with us, what will be the end of those who do not obey the gospel of God?

[18] And

"If the righteous man is scarcely
   saved,
where will the impious and sinner
   appear?"

[19]Therefore let those who suffer according to God's will do right and entrust their souls to a faithful Creator.

Most of the author's previous reflections on suffering now pass in review. The Christians should be the last to be "surprised" by the presence of suffering. The fate of Jesus and their own experience demonstrate that suffering is an intrinsic part of the Christian vocation. As the letter has repeatedly observed, such suffering has value. It is a "fiery ordeal" which "proves" the Christian. The author had discussed suffering as a "test" or "purification" in 1:6-7. Paradoxically, such suffering is even a cause for "rejoicing." This, too, had been discussed earlier in the letter. Suffering can bring joy because through it we share in Jesus' own redemptive work of bringing the world to glorify God (cf. 1:6-9; 2:21-25; 3:18).

The author never forgets the cost of discipleship. Part of that "cost" is the inner struggle to be free as we put to death our destructive desires (1:14; 2:11; 4:1-6). But the cost considered here (v.14) is suffering which comes from outside, from an uncomprehending and abusive world. This, too, has been a strong current in the epistle's message (2:12,15,18-25; 3:1-6,9,14,16; 4:4). As in 3:14, the author seems to invoke the beatitude of Matthew 5:11—to be "reproached for the name of Christ" is a "blessing." The source of that blessing is the Spirit. In a rather unusual formulation, the author describes the Spirit as "the spirit of glory and of God." "Glory" is one of 1 Peter's favorite themes (used ten times as a noun and four times as a verb). Traditionally the bible associates "glory" with God's awesome presence. When that presence is manifested "glory" streams out into the world. Conversely when humanity properly acknowledges God's presence, then this act of worship and praise is "glory" given to God. 1 Peter's use of the term fits into this perspective. He has linked the concept of glory to that final manifestation of God's saving presence which will be revealed at the end of the world (cf. 1:7; 4:13; 5:10). At that moment all of the world must respond by glorifying God. This is what 1 Peter has just affirmed (4:16; cf. 2:12; 4:11). Now he applies the term to the Spirit of God. This powerful source of life and strength flows from the God of glory who will be fully revealed at the end of time. But even now this Spirit of glory "rests upon" the Christians as they struggle and suffer courageously in their mission. That image of God's strengthening Spirit resting on the Christian seems to be drawn from the beautiful passage of Isaiah 11:2 where the Spirit of the Lord is described as "resting" on God's messiah, giving him a mission of justice. Now the Christians are God's agents of salvation, moving the world to glory.

Once again the author expresses his common sense conviction that not all suffering is worthwhile (4:15; cf. also 3:20). The just dues of being "a murderer or a thief, or a wrongdoer, or a mischief-maker"—a stock list of crimes—are not salvific, but to suffer "as a Christian" is another matter. The label "Christian" appears only three times in the New Testament, each time as a name given to the community by outsiders (cf. Acts 11:26; 26:28). 1 Peter has made it clear that the community was viewed with suspicion and hostility by the surrounding culture (cf. for example, 3:16; 4:4), therefore the name "Christian" probably has a contemptuous ring to it. But true to the spirit of his entire message, the author calls on his people to make such abuse an opportunity for glory rather than shame. "Suffering as a Christian"—that is, for leading a beautiful life even when society derides it—unites one to the work of the suffering Christ (cf. 2:21-25). Thus a name used with hostility by the pagans becomes a banner of glory for the believer.

A final dimension of suffering is brought forward, that of judgement (vv. 17-18). Twice before in the letter (2:8 and 4:5) the author had alluded to the pagans' accountability before God for the suffering they inflicted on the Christians. And in 1:17 he had reminded the Christians themselves that the God they called Father was also their judge. Judgement, in the sense of a final accountability, is a firm part of the New Testament tradition. On God's side, judgement is his ultimate act in the story of salvation. As a "just" God he is faithful to his promises—the struggle between good and evil, between life and death will not be left in doubt. God will act decisively to complete his work in the world. On humanity's part, judgement means the final outcome of our response to God's offer of salvation. The Bible uses a variety of imagery in its reflections on this final chapter of the world's story. When focusing on human responsibility it can use forensic images such as the great trial scene in Matthew 25:31-46. Some of Jesus' other parables move in a similar vein in speaking of judgement as a settling of accounts between a master and his servants (cf. Mt 24:45-51; 25:14-30). In other passages the drama of salvation is broadened out into a cosmic struggle between good and evil which is resolved by God's victory at the end of the world. This was a favorite theme of Jewish apocalyptic literature. The movement toward salvation is not a smooth evolution but a warfare, an agonizing struggle involving division, chaos, and even the apparent dissolution of the elements of nature. This kind of scenario is found in the New Testament in the Apocalypse and in portions of the Gospels (cf. Mk 13; Mt 24:1-44; Lk 21:5-36). Although some of this imagery may strike the modern reader as bizarre and should always be carefully interpreted in relation to the rest of the New Testament message, there is a fundamental truth involved here. The early Christians clung to their belief in God's power and goodness but they also had a healthy respect for sin and evil. The world was not an amusement park; the human capacity for destruction in which all share is real and evident. Therefore the ongoing work of salvation was a struggle, not an idyllic pilgrimage to glory. It calls for alertness and perseverance, for continuing responsibility.

These manifold dimensions of "judgement" are evoked by 1 Peter in verses 17 and 18. The sufferings endured by the Christians should be viewed from a cosmic perspective as part of the great drama of salvation. The author does not use the vivid imagery of apocalyptic tradition but his message is similar. The end time is near and it means a crisis for the community (v. 17). The Christians must be alert and responsive in this time of trial and suffering (cf. his exhortation in 4:7). But if the time of judgement spells crisis for the believers who are "God's household" (cf. the spirit of 2:4-10) all the more so for those "who do not obey the gospel of God." As in 2:8 and 3:1 the author seems to refer not to unbelievers in general but to those who have deliberately rejected the Christian message. Thus for 1 Peter the moment of judgement is not reserved for some spectacular forum at the end of the world but is already taking place in those deliberate choices of life or death which we consciously make in history. A quote from Proverbs 11:31 bolsters his argument: if salvation is a struggle for the "righteous" or faithful person, what will be the fate of the sinner? This threat of judgement for the unbeliever should be balanced with the author's words in 3:19-20 and 4:6 where he considers salvation from God's vantage point rather than from the perspective of human responsibility. Even the disobedience of Noah's contemporaries could not impede God's will to save. Jesus, the messenger of salvation, reached out to them in the prison of death itself! A sense of optimism and compassion rather than threat or condemnation is at the heart of 1 Peter's message.

Verse 19 concludes this whole section on suffering and does so in a spirit thoroughly typical of our author. The threat of suffering—whether as a purification, or a consequence of witness, or as part of the mysterious drama of judgement—must never immobilize the Christian with fear. Those who encounter pain "according to God's will" should "entrust their souls to a faithful Creator." The taproot of christian existence is complete trust in God; their "souls," that is, their entire lives (cf. 1:9), are in God's loving hands. This message has been repeated in practically every paragraph of 1 Peter's letter. This trust is the source of christian hope and the sustaining power of christian mission. The title "a faithful Creator" is found nowhere else in the New Testament but it beautifully expresses the vision of 1 Peter. The Christians were encouraged to participate in "created institutions" (2:13) because of the author's conviction that God was truly at work in the world, bringing his creative task to a glorious conclusion. So God is "faithful" to his promises inherent in creation itself—promises sensed by the prophets (1:10) but now experienced by the Christians. All of this should impel the Christian to "do right." In the Greek text of verse 19 these words conclude the sentence and stand in an emphatic position. All of the christians' convictions about God, about creation, about human destiny, about the meaning of suffering should lead them to persevere in their active witness of leading a good life.

AN EXHORTATION TO COMMUNITY LEADERS. 5:1-5.

5 So I exhort the elders among you, as a fellow elder and a witness of the sufferings of Christ as well as a partaker in the glory that is to be revealed. ²Tend the flock of God that is your charge, not by constraint but willingly, not for shameful gain but eagerly, ³not as domineering over those in your charge but being examples to the flock. ⁴And when the chief Shepherd is manifested you will obtain the unfading crown of glory. ⁵Likewise you that are younger be subject to the elders. Clothe yourselves, all of you, with humility toward one another, for "God opposes the proud, but gives grace to the humble."

1 Peter's exhortations have followed a set pattern: the witness of a courageously good life is linked to the discipline of inner freedom (2:11-12); the community's testimony of hope in the world is linked to the vigor of mutual love within the community (1:22; 3:8; 4:8). As the letter moves towards its finish, the author adds a third couplet: the community's fortitude in the midst of persecution and trial from without (4:12-19) is linked to the proper exercise of leadership within its boundaries (5:1-5). For the first time since the opening greeting (1:1) the author brings himself into the picture as he urges the leaders of the community to be good pastors and calls on the rest of the community to be responsive to their leadership. Although a number of New Testament books refer to various offices of leadership in the early church, information about the precise functions of these offices and the interrelationship of the various ranks is quite slim. This is because none of these texts are intended to be job descriptions but either a listing of the general qualities needed for office (as in 1 Tim 3:2-7, 8-13; Titus 1:5-9) or exhortations for carrying out the duties of office in the right spirit. The passage in 1 Peter falls into this latter category. Its form and tone are similar to the farewell speech of Paul to the "elders" of Ephesus (Acts 20:17-36). As 1 Peter does here, Paul invokes his own apostolic leadership and then encourages the elders to care for the "flock" in their charge.

The ones addressed are called "elders" (from the Greek word *presbyteros*). As the rest of the passage illustrates, Peter is not referring to the community's senior citizens but to a specific office of leadership. The term "elder" had this technical meaning in Judaism and in Greek culture. To bolster his own authority in advising this group, the author describes himself as a "fellow elder," as a "witness of the sufferings of Christ" and as "a partaker in the glory that is to be revealed." As we have already discussed in the Introduction and in connection with 1:1, it is not certain that the actual author of the letter is the apostle Peter. But it is also obvious that the author wishes to communicate these words as an instruction of Peter, the leader of the apostles, to those who share his ministry of leadership in the communities. It is interesting that despite this device the prerogatives cited by Peter are very general and, in fact, accessible to *all* the Christians. He is an "elder" that is, he holds an office of leadership; the writing of the epistle is itself an exercise of that office. He is a "witness" to Christ's sufferings, not in the sense of eyewitness to the passion (a boast quite unlikely in view of the gospel traditions about Peter's denial and desertion of Jesus during his passion); rather Peter shares in the common christian vocation of offering to the world a testimony of hope in the pattern of the suffering Christ (cf. 2:21; 4:1). He shares in the "glory to be revealed" just as every Christian has a stake in the great day of salvation (cf. 1:4-5).

The author uses pastoral imagery in offering his advice to the elders. Jesus was called the "Shepherd and Guardian" of the community in 2:25. Now that same image is applied to the community leadership. As we noted in discussing the shepherd title for Jesus (cf. above, 2:25), biblical tradition frequently used this as a metaphor for leadership, both good and bad. The sacredness of the elder's task rests on the fact that the community is "the flock of God." God's people deserve the very best.

Three sets of contrasting attitudes define what pastoral leadership should be. It must be exercised "willingly," not "by constraint." This implies that the office of leadership was conferred by designation or election. The one who was so chosen must not perform this service as a grim duty and his motivation must not be for money but "eagerly" (the word *prothumos* used here has the connotation of "wholeheartedly," with deep commitment). The elders were probably paid a salary and had charge of community finances. The list of qualities needed for "overseer" in 1 Timothy mentions their ability to manage and they are to be "no lovers of money (1 Tim 3:8; also Titus 1:7). These first two sets of qualities suggest that the leadership role in the early communities already had a significant degree of development. The third set is of a more general nature. The elders should not be "domineering over" the community but should be models or examples. The word for "domineering" (literally "lording it over") is the identical Greek word used in Mark 10:42 where Jesus decries the example of the pagan leaders who oppress their subjects and as "great ones" make their importance felt. To counter this example the Markan Jesus offers his own model of selfless service: "For the Son of Man also came not to be served but to serve, and to give his life as a ransom for many" (Mk 10:45). Through the way they exercise leadership, the elders can witness to the sufferings of Christ (cf. 5:1).

The reward held out to the leaders is the same vision that draws the entire community into the future: "the unfading crown of glory" (v.4). This share in glory will take place "when the chief Shepherd is manifested." In chapter 4 as in previous parts of the letter 1 Peter had sketched out the historical perspective of the believer: the old age of despair has given way to a time of hope (cf. especially 4:2-3,11,13). The Christians join with the suffering Christ in moving the world towards that moment of glory (2:12). By leading the community with integrity, with generosity, with compassion, the shepherds will be rewarded by the One who is the archetype of all church leadership.

The author follows through on his directives to the leaders with an appeal for cooperation from the rest of the community. The "younger" ones should be "subject to" the elders (v.5). The precise meaning of "younger" is not clear. Is the author referring to everyone who is not a leader, calling them "younger" in a figurative sense, playing off the word "elder"? Or does he mean it literally, recognizing that the younger members of the community either did or might have some difficulty with the authority figures? The fact that he goes on to address another category, "all of you," gives some support to the latter interpretation. In any case, the author calls on these "younger ones" to be subject to the elders. The verb "be subject to" is the same key word used in 2:13, 18, and 3:1 where the author discussed the community's involvement in society. Here as there the word does not connote blind obedience but the deliberate commitment to involve oneself in a societal institution "for the Lord's sake" (cf. the discussion under 2:13). the younger members of the community are asked to be involved in their church as an *institution* which means in this case being responsive to the legitimate authority of the leaders, even if such obedience does not come easily.

A final cast of the net brings in everyone, subjects and leaders: "clothe yourselves, all of you, with humility toward one another." The antidote for arrogance or resentment is "humility" (literally, "humble-mindedness"). This was not considered a virtue at all in hellenistic culture; only slaves had a right to be humble. But in Judaism and Christianity humility was a precious commodity. To be humble meant that one understood reality—the reality of God and our relationship to him. Recognition of our absolute dependence on God inevitably colors our image of ourselves and others. Only those blind to the reality of God could be deluded into the myth of their own self-sufficiency or into treating others without respect or compassion. In the hymn-like passage of Matthew 11:25-30, Jesus' own respect for insignificant people and his compassion for the burdened flow from his knowledge of God, from his "humility" (11:29). This is the attitude the members of the community should "clothe themselves with." A similar "clothing" metaphor is found in Colossians 3:12. But the particular word used by 1 Peter is unique in the New Testament. The *egkomboma* was a work apron or rough tunic used by slaves. So the Christians should strip off their illusions and face each other with a hearty sense of reality and, therefore, respect.

Following his usual pattern (cf. 1:24; 3:8; 4:18) the author seals off a series of exhortations with an Old Testament quotation. This verse from Proverbs 3:34 confirms the God-consciousness implied in the virtue of humility. The proud who act as if God did not exist are opposed by him, but the humble, who live by God's truth, receive his grace.

CONFIDENCE IN THE GOD OF ALL GRACE.
5:6-11.

> 6Humble yourselves therefore under the mighty hand
> of God, that in due time he may exalt you. 7Cast all your
> anxieties on him, for he cares about you. 8Be sober, be
> watchful. Your adversary the devil prowls around like a
> roaring lion, seeking some one to devour. 9Resist him,
> firm in your faith, knowing that the same experience of
> suffering is required of your brotherhood throughout the
> world. 10And after you have suffered a little while, the
> God of all grace, who has called you to his eternal glory
> in Christ, will himself restore, establish, and strengthen
> you. 11To him be the dominion for ever and ever. Amen.

As the author winds up his message he returns to his
starting point (cf. 1:3-5)—trust in the God who calls the
Christian to new life. That trust must not be shaken even as
the churches suffer on their way to glory. The whole passage
is very similar to James 4:6-10; both authors probably drew
on a common theme in early christian tradition.

The reference to humility in the previous verse (5) becomes the lead into this paragraph: the Christians are to
"humble" themselves "under the mighty hand of God" (v.6).
Humility, understood as a recognition of the truth about our
relationship to God (cf. our discussion of verse 5), can lead
only to confidence. The image of God's "mighty hand" does
not mean that the Christians are under God's thumb! This
expression is found in the Old Testament as an image of
God's power, especially his liberation of the people from
slavery in Egypt ("And the Lord brought us out of Egypt
with a mighty hand and an outstretched arm . . ." Deut 26:8).
To be "under God's hand" means protection and guidance
from a loving Father as one struggles to be free. Therefore,
the Christians can be confident that "in due time" he will
"exalt" them. This sense of optimism about the future is
a hallmark of 1 Peter's message.

The next verse (7) is a corollary to the preceding. The Christians should "cast off" or unburden all their anxieties on God because he "cares" for them. The mood of this verse, with its antithesis between anxiety and confidence in God's care, recalls one of the most exquisite passages of the Sermon on the Mount (cf. Mt 6:25-34). Anxiety about life is useless when one considers the loving care of God for his creation—for the birds of the air, for the lilies of the field, and far more precious than these, the human person. Throughout the epistle the author has displayed his awareness of the teaching of Jesus; many gospel sayings, including several from the Sermon on the Mount, have been blended into his text (cf. 3:9,14; 4:14). At the time 1 Peter was written these sayings may not yet have been fitted into the literary framework of a gospel; but they were part of the common fund of tradition handed on in the churches.

Confidence in God means more than casting our anxieties into his hands; it also gives the strength to be alert and active in the christian mission. For not only is God at work in history so is the "devil," the prince of evil. Therefore the Christians must be "sober" and "watchful." This call for readiness repeats what the author had said in 1:13 and 4:17. In these previous texts, sobriety and readiness were stances needed as God's saving word moves towards its climax at the end of the world. That endtime perspective is present in 5:8-9 but here the crisis atmosphere of the endtime is directly attributed to Satan. This reflects the healthy respect for evil that is part of biblical tradition (cf. the discussion under 4:17-18). Sin is not confined to the understandable world of individual human choice. Like some mysterious force it seeps out into all of our world, transcending our individual determinations and clutching human history in its vicious grasp. The modern world which has witnessed the horrors of two world wars, several genocides, and the continuing threat of nuclear holocaust, should feel a deep kinship with the cosmic scope of sin affirmed in the bible. One of the ways the New Testament describes this mystery is to recognize the agency of supra-human spirits behind the manifestations of evil in the world. Merely to dress Satan up in horns and tails and to place him under every bedpost makes this biblical tradition an easy target for modern skepticism and, in fact, misses the bible's insight about the mysterious transcendence of evil in human experience. That transcendence is respected neither by an exaggerated demonology nor by the romantic belief that all evil would go away if everyone enjoyed a good education.

1 Peter advises his Christians to draw on God's strength and to see evil as their "adversary." Evil is not passive but active; prowling the world like a roaring lion seeking the destruction of human life (the same aggressive image of evil is found in Dan 7:4-7 and 2 Tim 4:17; it is also used in some of the Qumran writings). Therefore the Christians must "resist" (v.9) using the strength of their faith in God. In the opening lines of the letter, the author had spoken of faith in a similar context of testing and endurance (cf. 1:5-8). Here the Christians are urged to recall not only their communion with God but also their fellowship in faith and suffering with the church "throughout the world" (v.9). This consciousness of a world-wide church is indicative of the mission perspective of 1 Peter. The sufferings endured by the local community are not isolated irritants but intrinsic to the experience of being a follower of Jesus; and by the same token, the bearing of suffering "as a Christian" (4:16) is part of a cosmic transformation in which the power of evil will be overcome and the world will find its way to God.

That is the spirit of the final verses (10-11) in this concluding section. Themes orchestrated throughout the letter crescendo in a triumphant and sustained chord. The author's convictions about the meaning of suffering, about human faith, about the identity and destiny of the Christians are melded into a firm promise. "After you have suffered a little while"—history is shot through with suffering but it is on its way to glory, an end that is not far off (cf. 4:7). "The God of all grace"—the Father of Jesus has revealed himself as a loving giver of "grace" to the community; the gift of salvation (1:10,13; 3:7), the gift of suffering (2:19-20), the gifts of service and love (4:10-11). This gracious God is the one who called the Christians to share his glory "in Christ" (cf. above 3:16). And that call is not in vain. After a short time of redemptive suffering, this good God will "restore, establish, and strengthen" those called. God's people in exile, broken and scattered, will be brought home and made whole (cf. 1:1; 2:11). Faced with such a God and with such care for his world, only one response is right: "to him be the dominion for ever and ever. Amen" (v.11; cf. also 4:11).

FINAL WORD.
5:12-14.

¹²By Silvanus, a faithful brother as I regard him, I have written briefly to you, exhorting and declaring that this is the true grace of God; stand fast in it. ¹³She who is at Babylon, who is likewise chosen, sends you greetings; and so does my son Mark. ¹⁴Greet one another with the kiss of love.
Peace to all of you that are in Christ.

The letter concludes with some comments about the origin and purpose of the letter and with a warm greeting to the churches. Even though these lines are brief, they are typical of the letter's rich spirit.

The author mentions that the letter was written "by Silvanus, a faithful brother as I regard him" (v.12). As mentioned in the Introduction to the commentary, it is hard to be sure what "by" really means here. At face value, it would seem to indicate that Silvanus was either Peter's secretary helping to compose the letter or the messenger who carried the letter to the churches of Asia Minor. But it is our contention that Silvanus along with Peter was an important *source* for the letter's message rather than the immediate writer or bearer of the text. Although the author uses the device of pseudonymity (cf. Introduction), what he says about Silvanus is true. Peter's message comes to the churches of Asia Minor *through the medium* of one of Peter's trusted associates, Silvanus—and more proximately through the author who was able to draw on these and other christian traditions in Peter's name.

The stated purpose of the letter fits what we have discovered about its style and message: the author "declares" (literally, "testifies') what is the "true grace of God" and "exhorts" the Christians to "stand fast in it." 1 Peter's brilliant and inspiring description of the christian vocation in the world shows that the author achieved his purpose well. The fact that the letter was made part of the New Testament indicates that the early church agreed with this verdict.

The letter comes from "Babylon," a word used in first-century Jewish literature and in the book of the Apocalypse (cf. 14:8; 17:5,18; 18:2) as a code name for Rome. The choice of name shows the critical stance of the Christians toward the city and world power that dominated their cultural and political life. "Babylon" spelled aggression and exile for those familiar with biblical history. Although 1 Peter has called for full participation in civil and social life (cf. 2:13-17), he does not wink at the vastly different philosophies of life that separated this worldly power from the Kingdom of God.

The church at Rome shares in the same call and destiny as the churches who will receive this letter: it, too, is "chosen" (cf. 2:9-10). And now from this church set in the heart of the Roman world greetings go out to small towns in the outback provinces of Asia Minor. No other New Testament book gives such explicit evidence of the strong bonds among the early communities of the church (cf. Introduction). One of the prominent members of the Roman church and a close companion (the sense of "my son") of Peter is Mark (5:13). This is undoubtedly an authentic historical reference to the same prominent Christian and early missionary mentioned in several New Testament passages (cf. Acts 12:12-17 where he is mentioned with Peter; 12:25 and 13:5 with Barnabas and Paul; with Barnabas in Acts 15:36-41; and with Paul in

Col 4:10 [where the apostle mentions that Mark is a cousin of Barnabas], Philemon 24; 2 Tim 4:11). Later tradition assigned the authorship of the gospel that bears his name to this same companion of Peter.

On the receipt of the letter, the Christians are to "greet one another with the kiss of love" (v.14). In Greek culture the kiss was an accepted greeting of friendship. For the Christians, bound together by a common call, a common faith and a common destiny, the "kiss of love" was to be no perfunctory ritual but a joyous expression of their identity as God's people.

The author leaves his Christians with the gift that belongs to those "in Christ" (cf. 3:16). People whose hope is based on Christ, who pattern their lives of witness on the crucified and risen Jesus—to these "peace" belongs.

*Commentary
on 2 Peter*

INTRODUCTION
TO 2 PETER

MANY MODERN READERS will not be attracted to the
Second Letter of Peter. Its combative tone, its rather abstract description of christian life and its dire warnings of
world destruction make it, for some, an ugly duckling in the
New Testament flock. 2 Peter competes with Jude for being
the least read and least appreciated of biblical books.

But this verdict is unfortunate. 2 Peter should be read not
simply out of respect for the fact that it is part of the inspired scriptures but also because beneath the veneer of its
unattractive language is a gospel message the contemporary
church could afford to hear.

The Occasion of the Letter

As noted in the general Introduction, 2 Peter was not
written by the apostle. An author writing long after Peter's
death, perhaps as late as 125 A.D., uses the name of the
apostle to ram home his message about authentic tradition
and to justify his right to speak in strong tones to his sister
churches. The letter does not mention its specific point of
origin nor does it identify the churches to which it is sent.
The fact that it invokes the name of Peter and refers to the
first letter of Peter (1:1; 3:1) suggests it was written from
Rome to the same general region of northern Asia Minor as
1 Peter was. The author uses the format of a letter or epistle
common in many of the New Testament writings, but other
literary forms seem to influence the style of the work as a
whole. The author presents Peter as giving a solemn message

to his fellow Christians as he himself is about to depart from life (cf. 1:12-15). This gives the letter the tone of a "valedictory," a common literary form in the ancient world whereby a great leader leaves a final testimony to his community of followers (cf. Paul and the Pastoral Letters or even the final discourse of Jesus in Jn 13-17). Some recent scholars detect the influence of a literary form known as the "civic decree," an official text in which a benefactor documents his favors to the recipients. The influence of these literary forms helps explain some of the stiff and formal character of 2 Peter.

The author wrote this epistle because the very life of the christian community was under threat. The direct source of that threat was not the Roman state nor, as in the case of 1 Peter, a hostile environment. It was a threat from within. Influential members of the community were preaching a false gospel and living a counterfeit christian life. Their teaching and example were seducing other members of the community, especially new converts (2:18). The letter gives us some idea of what the false teachers were up to. They ridiculed belief in the second coming of the Lord by maintaining that the world and its history were not moving towards any final destiny. All of creation was doomed to an eternal treadmill. The "delay" of the expected parousia—the delay that had taken the community past the lifetime of its first generation of believers (3:4-5)—only bolstered the contention of these teachers and enabled them to taunt the community: "Where is the promise of his coming?" (3:4). These same teachers also led lives of promiscuity, claiming to be "free" of ordinary moral restraints. They boasted about their superior knowledge and cleverly exploited other Christians, apparently using their powers for their own economic profit (2:14-15). Some of these symptoms are similar to those of the gnostic heretics that would plague the church in the later second and third centuries. But we cannot be sure if there is any connection between the two groups.

The assault of the false teachers was compounded by the cultural atmosphere in which the Christians had to live. This period of history was marked by religious scepticism. Traditional religions and philosophical convictions about the existence of God and human immortality were ridiculed by many of the intellectual elite of Greco-Roman society. The religious vacuum created by the collapse of traditional religion in the empire was filled by a host of trendy oriental cults and by a popular thirst for exotic religious experience. Many people shopped around for new religions, often being involved in several at one time. Judaism and christianity were exceptional in their demands for exclusive religious commitment and for a strong moral code. It takes little imagination to appreciate the difficulties the early church had in surviving such an atmosphere. The thoroughly gentile converts of the church addressed in this letter had little grounding and therefore made easy targets for the subtle errors of false teachers.

The Message of the Letter

The vehemence of 2 Peter's response to all this is not explained simply by a concern for keeping people in the fold. The false teachers' denial of a destiny for creation and their promiscuity—all in the name of a "superior" christianity—represented a fundamental distortion of the gospel. It was this mortal threat to the gospel—and not just a threat to membership—that drew the fire of our author.

His reponse is on two fronts. First of all he reminds the Christians that his own viewpoint is backed up by sound tradition, a tradition that stretches back to the apostles (represented in the letter by Peter himself) and ultimately to Jesus who is imbued with God's own power and glory (1:16-19) and who remains the "Lord and Savior" of the church. The basic outlines of that tradition are quickly sketched by the author: God's mercy as the source of our salvation (1:3-4); Jesus as the revelation of God's goodness and the agent of our redemption (1:16-19); the call to conversion and holiness (3:11-12,14,18); the great promise of "a new heavens and a new earth" (1:4; 3:13). One of the hallmarks of 2 Peter is the description of this tradition in language understandable to his gentile Christians. To a greater degree than any other New Testament author, 2 Peter casts biblical and Jewish concepts into more abstract Greek terms. This process of re-interpretation is a positive sign of the author's sensitivity to his people. 2 Peter's insistence on authority and tradition should not be interpreted as the knee jerk of an ecclesiastical mentality. There are some kinds of aberrations wrapped in the cloak of religion that deserve to be exposed to the glare of time-tested christian belief and practice.

The author's second front is a direct assault on the false teachers themselves. 2 Peter borrows heavily from the letter of Jude for this task (cf., especially, 2 Pt chapter 2). The language burns with indignation and spares little in ravaging the teacher's errors. Such language might seem offensive to modern Christians. Our sensitivity may be well founded, but there may also be occasions when prophetic rage at the violation of the truth is not only justified but called for. After all, Jude and 2 Peter had a precedent in Jesus' own violent attacks on false teaching in the gospels. Still this kind of blistering denunciation should be rare and used cautiously lest our righteous anger mask nothing more than verbal revenge or a sense of false superiority.

The Letter Today

The qualities of 2 Peter enunciated above are worth consideration by the contemporary church. Religious hokum in the name of the gospel has not gone away. Nor are we strangers to a kind of religious fanaticism that can lead to catastrophe for those caught in its force. There are times and events that do not allow authentic christian leadership to remain silent. And we, too, need to be convinced of a future for humanity with an intensity equal to that of 2 Peter.

His warnings about a destruction by fire may not be an apt metaphor for our times, but we as much as the early christians need to resist any absolute claims for human invention and to remain faithful to the vision of a "new heavens and a new earth," which only the Spirit of God can create. Finally, 2 Peter's attempts to recast traditional biblical metaphors into more philosophical or abstract knowledge reminds us that a rigid adherence to literal biblical language is not even the spirit of the scriptures themselves.

Part I.

The Power of God's Promises

1:1-21.

This first major section is the most positive part of the letter. The author plunges immediately into his statement of basic christian belief and stresses his own apostolic authority. His concern with false teaching is barely concealed (cf. 1:9,16,20-31); it will erupt in the next two sections.

GREETINGS.
1:1-2.

> **1** Simeon Peter, a servant and apostle of Jesus Christ,
> To those who have obtained a faith of equal standing with ours in the righteousness of our God and Savior Jesus Christ:
> ²May grace and peace be multiplied to you in the knowledge of God and of Jesus our Lord.

The author begins with the standard format of a Greek letter. Even in these initial words the formal and somewhat stiff tone of 2 Peter is apparent. As is the case with the greetings of several New Testament letters, major themes to be taken up in the body of the work are already detectable.

The author identifies himself as "Simeon Peter, a servant and apostle of Jesus Christ." As suggested in the Introduction it is highly unlikely that Peter wrote the letter. "Simeon" is a more literal rendering of the Hebrew name *Shimon* and is rare in the New Testament (cf. Acts 15:14); it may reflect the real author's attempt to give a certain ring of authenticity to the letter. Peter is called a "servant" stressing his share in the common christian vocation to serve as Jesus did, but he is also an "apostle," a singular role of leadership exercised by the first followers of Jesus and the earliest missionaries (Paul stresses his claim to the title under this latter heading). Unlike 1 Peter, the author of this letter will repeatedly stress the unique authority of Peter as a privileged and authentic witness to Jesus. One reason for this emphasis on authority is the very purpose of 2 Peter which is to oppose false teachers in the community.

The addressees are left unidentified. On the basis of 3:1 where the author refers to this as "the second letter" sent to the Christians, one can presume that the audiences are generally the same in both cases, namely, the christian communities of Asia Minor (cf. 1 Pt 1:1). The generalized address of 2 Peter fits into its more impersonal style and its form as a "valedictory" or "decree" intended for wider circulation in the communities (cf. Introduction). The only label given to the recipients is that they "have obtained a faith of equal standing" with Peter. "Faith" as used here takes on a different nuance than the basic idea of trust that it usually has in Paul's writings or in 1 Peter. While not excluding this deeper meaning, the "faith" 2 Peter refers to is the whole spectrum of christian existence, including understanding of authentic christian tradition and participation in the life of the community. The equality or "equal standing" that the Christians enjoy with Peter is a result of the "righteousness" (or, more literally, the "justice") of Jesus. Through his redemptive work Jesus has brought to all Christians the experience of God's merciful fidelity; fidelity is the basic meaning of God's "justice" in biblical literature and it seems to retain that meaning here.

The title given to Jesus in verse 1 is significant: "our God and Savior Jesus Christ." Although some scholars prefer to translate this as a double reference—i.e., our God (the Father) and our Savior (Jesus)—it is more probable that 2 Peter applies the title "God" to Jesus. A few other New Testament texts also call Jesus "God": cf. John 20:28; Titus

2:13; Hebrews 1:8 and possibly Romans 9:5. As the early community deepened its reflection on Jesus' divine power it had less hesitation in applying such a title directly to him. Other Old Testament titles for God were applied to Jesus even at an early stage in christian reflection (cf. for example, the title "Lord" in Phil 2:11). 2 Peter likes to pair titles for Jesus and that is the case here where he is called "God and Savior." "Savior," too, was an attribute of Yahweh in the Old Testament and is used of Jesus in a number of New Testament texts to express the Christians' conviction that through Jesus they had experienced the saving power of God (cf. Lk 2:11; Jn 4:42; Eph 5:23; Phil 3:20; 1 Jn 4:14).

Even though 2 Peter states his equality with the rest of the Christians in this opening verse he does not hesitate to address them with a strong tone of authority in the rest of the letter. "Equality" does not mean that every interpretation is acceptable or that any type of conduct is authentic christian living.

The greeting continues with a blessing (v.2) that is very similar to that of 1 Peter 1:2. A significant addition is the word "knowledge." Throughout the letter the author will stress sound teaching and right knowledge (cf. below, 1:3). Fidelity to the meaning of the gospel is what will guarantee the blessings of grace and peace.

THE POWER OF HIS PROMISES.
1:3-4.

> [3]His divine power has granted to us all things that pertain to life and godliness, through the knowledge of him who called us to his own glory and excellence, [4]by which he has granted to us his precious and very great promises, that through these you may escape from the corruption that is in the world because of passion, and become partakers of the divine nature.

These two verses are characteristic of 2 Peter. They are complicated grammatically, fitting into the rather sophisticated language and abstract concepts of the author. And some of the key terms found here are drawn from secular Greek culture rather than from biblical or Jewish traditions—another significant trademark of 2 Peter. The basic ideas expressed are at the heart of the letter's message.

The grammatical problems can be tackled first, although no definite solution can be found for them. The participial construction of the verb in verse 3 suggests that this segment is actually a continuation of the preceding verse, a reflection on the meaning of the term "knowledge" in order to lay the groundwork for the exhortations that will begin in verse 5. The undefined pronouns—"him" and "us"—also cause some difficulties. Is "he" referring to God throughout or at some point (as in "him who called us") does the author intend to refer to Jesus? Parallel to this, is the "us" referring to Christians in general or to Peter and the apostles in particular? Although some commentators take a different route, we prefer to understand "he" as referring to God (and not specifically referring to Jesus) and "us" as referring to all Christians.

The passage dwells on the benefits which true knowledge of God brings to the Christians. These benefits are granted to us by God's "divine power." It is typical of 2 Peter to use such abstract expressions to refer to what is quite personal, in this case God himself. God has given to baptized Christians everything that pertains to "life and godliness." The latter term in Greek is *eusebeia*, a general word for goodness and piety.

The next phrase specifies the medium of these gifts— "through the knowledge of him who called us to his own glory and excellence." As in verse 2, the author reveals his affinity with Greek culture by emphasizing "knowledge." The connotation of the word throughout 2 Peter is not simply abstract knowledge of God, but a deep awareness of God through Jesus and a fidelity to the christian tradition. This kind of "knowledge" expresses itself in right conduct.

Thus the word has a comprehensiveness to it that might not be apparent at first.

The one known is the God who "called us"; here the author evokes a more traditional biblical motif. From Abraham to Paul, God's people have treasured their sense of being called from darkness to life. Due to variants in the early manuscripts, it is not certain whether the author says we are called *to* or *by* God's own "glory and excellence." "Glory" is used in biblical tradition as a quasi-technical term for a manifestation of God's presence in history (cf. 1 Peter 4:14). "Excellence" translates the Greek term *arete* and means virtue or acts of power. Either the author wants to say that we are called *to share in* God's divine nature and power (as he will explicitly state in v.4), or that *by means of* his glory and excellence we have been called. The opening words of the next verse continue the baffling vagueness. "By which" probably refers to "glory and excellence," but it could reach back to "all things."

Some clarity returns when the author moves on to another biblical image, that of "promise" (v.4). The entire bible lives in an atmosphere of promise. The people of Israel move toward the future confident that their longings for wholeness and new life—longings imbedded in them by God—will be fulfilled. The Christians see Jesus as the fulfillment of the promises made to Israel and as the revealer of even more staggering promises by God.

The promise of eternal life revealed through the resurrection of Jesus seems to be the key concern of 2 Peter. Through God's "precious and very great promises" the Christians escape the "corruption" of this world and become "partakers of the divine nature" (v.4). Both ends of the redemptive process are described in typically hellenistic language. Some strands of religious thought in the hellenistic world longed for "deification." Through "knowledge" one could shed corrupt human nature and participate in the life of the gods. This sharing in "divine nature" primarily meant achieving immortality. In the New Testament period these religious ideas were not accepted by everyone and were even the target of much scepticism and ridicule by the educated elite of the pagan world. Our author walks a fine line in using terminology familiar to the gentile Christians of Asia Minor from their pagan background, while, at the same time, reinterpreting these ideas in the light of sound christian tradition. Thus he does not brand the "world" or human nature as totally corrupt—something that would be contrary to the biblical view of creation and to the heart of the gospel. He carefully says: "corruption that is in the world *because of passion*" (v.4). By "passion" he means the kind of unbridled desires that are the result of sin (cf. a similar use of the word in 1 Peter 1:14; 2:11). The world is a crippled beauty: a gift of God yet laced with the reality of sin. The other end of the redemptive process is described as participation in the "divine nature." This is the only occurence of this abstract term in the bible. 2 Peter does not mean to imply that we become divine beings or demi-gods; he has already strongly affirmed that salvation is a *gift* of God in preceding verses and he will do so again in the letter. Rather, we share in the "divine nature" by being called by God to the destiny of unending life with him (cf. 1:10-11).

These two verses introduce us to one of the special talents of 2 Peter. Throughout the letter the author attempts to translate the christian message into non-biblical concepts. Terms such as "divine," "life and godliness," "knowledge," "excellence," "corruption," "divine nature" are all non-christian religious and philosophical terminology. The result of the "translation" process is that 2 Peter can seem less warm and more abstract than other New Testament works; yet the importance of what he attempted should not be overlooked. This work stands in the vanguard of a process of interpretation that stretches to our own day.

FAITH IN ACTION.
1:5-11.

[5]For this very reason make every effort to supplement your faith with virtue, and virtue with knowledge, [6]and

knowledge with self-control, and self-control with steadfastness, and steadfastness with godliness, [7]and godliness
with brotherly affection, and brotherly affection with
love. [8]For if these things are yours and abound, they keep
you from being ineffective or unfruitful in the knowledge
of our Lord Jesus Christ. [9]For whoever lacks these things
is blind and shortsighted and has forgotten that he was
cleansed from his old sins. [10]Therefore, brethren, be the
more zealous to confirm your call and election, for if you
do this you will never fall; [11]so there will be richly provided for you an entrance into the eternal kingdom of our
Lord and Savior Jesus Christ.

Having reminded the Christians of their glorious destiny
with God (1:3-4), the author now urges them to live out
their faith. This is a typical pattern in the New Testament:
first the encouraging good news, then the call to live in a
way worthy of the gospel. 2 Peter casts his appeal in a framework typical of Greco-Roman ethical literature. A string of
virtues are linked together, mounting up to the most important and comprehensive (cf. an example of this in Rom
5:3-8). Not only the form but the content of 2 Peter's list
offers continuing evidence of his desire to translate christian
teaching into concepts familiar to his gentile audience.
Terms such as "virtue," "knowledge," "self-control," "godliness" are typical in Greek and Roman literature but relative-
ly rare in biblical writings. At the same time, the author is
not a prisoner of these literary patterns: the virtues selected
fit the overall message of the letter and the movement of the
list from "faith" to "love" is thoroughly christian.

Verse 5 states the author's thesis: "for this very reason"—
because we have been granted God's promise of eternal
life—we should express our faith in action. This is the concern of the entire passage. The actions or "virtues" (the
same word *arete* used of God in v.3) singled out begin with
"knowledge." Unlike the intensive form of the word *epi-
gnosis*, used in verses 2, 3, and 8, "knowledge" *(gnosis)* here
probably has the more limited sense of knowing good from

evil. "Self-control" may be mentioned in anticipation of the troublemakers in the community who are notably lacking in this virtue (cf. chapter 2). "Steadfastness" or perseverance may also be included because of the problems taken up later in the epistle, namely impatience with the coming of the parousia (cf. chapter 3). "Godliness" or piety was already cited in 1:3; the false teachers will be labeled "ungodly" in 2:6 and 3:7. The climax of the list is love—love for members of the community (*philadelphia* here is translated as "brotherly affection") and the more universal love of the Christians for their neighbors (*agape* translated simply as "love"). The centering of all christian demands on that of love is the heart of the gospel (cf. a similar pattern in 1 Peter 3:8; 4:8).

The author rounds out his exhortations by restating— positively and negatively—his basic premise. To exercise these basic virtues prevents the christian vocation from being "ineffective or unfruitful." Once again the author describes christian life in typically Greek concepts as "knowledge of our Lord Jesus Christ" (v.8). This whole section demonstrates that by "knowledge" he means not an intellectual exercise but a dynamic relationship with Christ that transforms our entire lives. To lead an unfruitful life is to be "blind" and to forget the meaning of one's baptism (described as "cleansing from old sins"; cf. similar terminology in 1 Peter 1:22, as well as 1 Cor 6:11; Eph 5:26; Titus 3:5). The same thesis is restated, positively, in verses 10 and 11. The "brethren" should strive to "confirm (their) call and election" by expressing their faith in action. The notion of christian life as a "call" or "choice" by God is widespread in the New Testament (cf. for example, 1 Peter 1:15; 2:2). In so doing the Christians avoid a "fall." By this the author probably means not ordinary sins or failings but the definitive loss of salvation (cf. a similar idea in Jude 24, one of the many instances where 2 Peter draws on this earlier work). The outcome of a life filled with virtue is "entrance into the eternal Kingdom of our Lord and Savior Jesus Christ" (v.11). The image of "entering the Kingdom of God" is found in the synoptic gospels as a way of describing conversion (cf. for example, Mt 10:23). But here the term "Kingdom *of Christ*" (cf. also Eph 5:5; Col 1:13; 2 Tim 4:1) is used instead of the more common "Kingdom of God." Paul speaks of "Christ's Kingdom" as an interim period before the final day (1 Cor 15:24) but in 2 Peter it refers to the ultimate stage of salvation itself, when the Christians will be united with God through the power of their "Lord and Savior." This couplet of titles so common in contemporary Christianity is found in the New Testament only in 2 Peter (cf. 2:20; 3:2,18).

PETER'S TESTAMENT.
1:12-15.

> [12]Therefore I intend always to remind you of these things, though you know them and are established in the truth that you have. [13]I think it right, as long as I am in this body, to arouse you by way of reminder, [14]since I know that the putting off of my body will be soon, as our Lord Jesus Christ showed me. [15]And I will see to it that after my departure you may be able at any time to recall these things.

Having summoned up the vision of christian destiny and called for an active faith, the author now reflects on his purpose in writing the letter. Unlike 1 Peter where the role of the apostle intruded rarely into the message of the letter, in 2 Peter the apostolic testimony of the supposed author is given a prominent place.

Peter's goal is to "remind" the Christians of "these things," presumably their vocation and the responsibilities that flow from it. "Reminding" the community of its heritage was a major goal of early christian exhortation (cf. Jude 5). The author flatters his readers by conceding that they already "know this and are established in the truth that you have" (v. 12). However, as the letter progresses it is obvious that the author is anxious about how "established" the Christians really are in their faith.

The author alludes in somewhat poetic language to his own impending death (vv.13-14). This gives the entire letter the mood of a valedictory or farewell testament as the leader of the apostles hands on to his Christians a last exhortation about their faith (cf. Paul in Acts 20:17-38 and 2 Tim 3:1–4:8). He speaks of death as "putting off of my body"; the word used in the Greek text is "tent." The description of bodily existence as a "tent" is fairly common in Greek literature and is found in a few biblical passages (cf. 2 Cor 6:1; Wis 9:15). The Lord Jesus Christ had revealed to the apostle that his death would come soon (v.14). This might reflect a tradition similar to that in John 21:18-19 where Jesus predicts Peter's martyrdom. Another possible tradition is the famous *Quo Vadis* scene from the *Acts of Peter*, a late second century writing. While some contact with these or other traditions cannot be ruled out, it is more likely that the author is simply utilizing the reader's knowledge that Peter *had been* martyred. It was an acceptable part of the pseudonymous writing technique that the hero would predict a future event that the reader knew had already happened. This allowed the author to interpret the meaning of now historical events. So here, the Lord has made known to Peter that he must "depart" but his legacy to the church will continue in the testament he now sends to the churches. In reading this exhortation the later generations of Christians will be in contact with the authentic christian tradition handed on by the apostle.

THE SURE PROPHETIC WORD.
1:16-21.

[16]For we did not follow cleverly devised myths when we made known to you the power and coming of our Lord Jesus Christ, but we were eyewitnesses of his majesty. [17]For when he received honor and glory from God the Father and the voice was borne to him by the Majestic Glory, "This is my beloved Son, with whom I am well pleased," [18]we heard this voice borne from heaven, for we were with him on the holy mountain. [19]And we have

the prophetic word made more sure. You will do well to pay attention to this as to a lamp shining in a dark place, until the day dawns and the morning star rises in your hearts. [20]First of all you must understand this, that no prophecy of scripture is a matter of one's own interpretation, [21]because no prophecy ever came by the impulse of man, but men moved by the Holy Spirit spoke from God.

As the author gears up for his attack on the false teachers (cf. chapter 2) he reassures the readers about the reliability of his own apostolic teaching.

The tradition handed on to the Christians by the apostles (the "we" in v.16) was not "cleverly devised myths" but the testimony of "eyewitnesses." Apparently some Christians had begun to ridicule belief in the Second Coming of Jesus, branding it as a fable or "myth" (cf. 3:3-13; the word is used in a pejorative sense in 1 Tim 1:4; 4:7; 2 Tim 4:4; Titus 1:14). The "power and coming" of Jesus refer not to his incarnation but his return in glory at the end of the world. Peter uses a technical word *parousia* for "coming," a term applied to Jesus' glorious return (cf. Mt 24:3; 1 Cor 15:23; 1 Thess 2:14; 2 Thess 2:8; Jas 5:7-8; 1 Jn 2:28). Peter counters the ridicule of the opponents by stressing the basis of his authority and the resulting nature of christian tradition. Christianity is not a clever fable but is rooted in history, in the person of Jesus and in those spirit-filled witnesses who experienced his power.

The event that best illustrates the origin and authority of the tradition for 2 Peter is the transfiguration. This event serves the author's purpose because not only does it illustrate Jesus' "majesty" but it incorporates the witness role of Peter and the guaranteeing words of God himself. Jesus' "majesty" consists in the fact that he in an absolutely unique way partakes in the "honor and glory" of God (1:16-17; cf. the promise to the Christians in 1:3-4). Jesus' own authority and mission are ratified by the Father's word: "This is my beloved Son with whom I am well pleased" (words almost

identical to the account in Mt 17:5). The message is borne
to Jesus by "the Majestic Glory," a circumlocution for
the name of God used in late Judaism.

The apostles who witnessed these events in turn now share
in the authority of Jesus. They have "heard the voice" and
they were "with (Jesus) on the holy mountain" (v. 18). The
mount of transfiguration is viewed as a sacred place so
2 Peter uses language reminiscent of the biblical terms for
Mount Zion (cf. Ps 2:6) where the temple and the city of
Jerusalem were based—a place of God's presence and his
revelation to Israel. The apostles' experience of these events
makes their prophetic message "more sure." The term
"prophetic word" (v. 19) probably refers to the entire
Hebrew scriptures which were the early church's bible. The
Christians viewed all of the scriptures as a "prophecy" of
Jesus and the climactic work of salvation he would inaugurate (cf. our discussion of 1 Peter 1:10). Some commentators
suggest that 2 Peter had in mind a more specific Old Testament passage such as Numbers 24:17 or Daniel 7:13-14, both
of which were interpreted as predicting the second coming
of Christ. Although teaching about the parousia is a major
issue for the author there is no way of being sure he had
these specific scripture passages in view.

The authenticity of the apostolic witness now leads to
some caveats about interpretation—the author's diatribe
against the false teachers is beginning to boil to the surface
(cf. 2:1). The "prophetic word" as handed on in the apostles'
testimony and in the authentic tradition of the community
must be respected. This properly interpreted word is a"lamp
shining in a dark place," a light that will sustain the Christians in history until the end of the world. That end is described in beautifully poetic language: "when the day
dawns"—a biblical image used generally for the coming of
salvation (cf. Lk 1:78) or for the parousia (cf. Rom 13:12);
when "the morning star rises in your hearts"—the star image
was applied in Judaism and early christianity to the Messiah
on the basis of Numbers 24:17 (cf. Mt 2:2). Apocalypse 22:16

speaks of Jesus as "the bright morning star." 2 Peter is obviously drawing on this biblical tradition but the word he uses for "morning star" is *phosphoros*, the word for the planet Venus and the Greek gods Artemis and Hecate. This is another instance of the author's adaptation of biblical tradition into concepts drawn from secular culture. This "morning star" will dispel the darkness of the human heart, an emphasis on the personal transformation to take place in the endtime that contrasts with the violent apocalyptic imagery used later in the letter (cf. 3:7,10,11-12).

Respecting God's prophetic word means avoiding superficial interpretations of it (vv.20-21). No prophecy can be merely "one's own interpretation" or "by the impulse of man." Only those who are animated by the Holy Spirit can give a genuine interpretation of God's word. This is not an argument against personal reading and reflection on scripture. Rather, the author had in mind the "false prophets" who were diluting the gospel (cf. 3:3-13) and twisting Paul's teaching on freedom (3:14-17). By cutting themselves off from the authentic life and tradition of the community these "false teachers" showed they were not imbued with the Spirit of God. Their inauthenticity is the major concern of next part of the letter.

Part II.

The Treachery of False Teachers
2:1-22.

The problems that triggered the letter are exposed in this major section. "False teachers" are leading the community into serious error and sapping its moral strength. To snap his readers to attention about this mortal compromise of their faith the author unleashes a violent denunciation of these teachers. It is important to remember the situation of isolated gentile communities in the era of 2 Peter. The world in which they lived was confused and sceptical about religious belief. Traditional religions had long since broken down. A large segment of the educated classes in the empire were cynical about the possibility of the transcendent. Others sought meaning by shopping around in various religious trends such as the mystery cults or other Eastern religions. Not a few were curious about Judaism itself. Except for Judaism and christianity, few of these religions made any claims for exclusivity; their adherents were free to dabble in several cults at the same time.

It is easy to understand how some members of a christian community could be swamped by this atmosphere of stark secularity and religious confusion. This would be especially true if a community came under the sway of some clever and articulate "teachers" who could deftly ridicule the community's beliefs and scandalize its weaker members with a "free" life-style. There are situations when the allure of such religious hokery becomes not just an irritant but a serious threat to the very center of christian faith. A generation who has witnessed the unspeakable tragedy of

Jonestown should need no persuasion on this point. This seems to be the kind of serious threat that provokes 2 Peter's diatribe.

Throughout this section he borrows from the Letter of Jude. As the commentary will indicate, the author adapts Jude 4-16 to fit the situation of this letter. Where Jude seems more concerned with the moral misbehavior, 2 Peter broadens this to include doctrinal aberrations, especially teaching about eschatology. And whereas Jude can count on his reader's acquaintance with certain non-biblical Jewish writings dealing with the end of the world (e.g., Enoch), 2 Peter cannot make such suppositions about his thoroughly gentile audience.

THE RISE OF FALSE TEACHERS.
2:1-3.

> 2 But false prophets also arose among the people, just as there will be false teachers among you, who will secretly bring in destructive heresies, even denying the Master who bought them, bringing upon themselves swift destruction. ²And many will follow their licentiousness, and because of them the way of truth will be reviled. ³And in their greed they exploit you with false words; from of old their condemnation has not been idle, and their destruction has not been asleep.

The first part of his attack warns the community about the coming threat of false teachers. The "last testament" nature of the whole letter makes this a warning about a *future* threat. But for the actual author of the letter and his audience that threat had already come true. In verses 10-22 the author sheds this literary fiction and speaks in the present tense.

The coming of false teachers is compared to the "false prophets" that afflicted the people of Israel (v. 1). The Hebrew scriptures had minced no words about them (cf. Jer 2:9; 8-9; Dt 18:20-21; etc.). Other New Testament writings railed against "false prophets" who abused God's word, and considered them as part of the struggles to be endured in the final age (cf. Mk 13:22; Mt 24:11). Adapting verse 4 of the Letter of Jude, our author describes these teachers as people who smuggle "destructive heresies" into the community. "Heresy" is a Greek term for a school of thought; in Paul's writings as here in 2 Peter it loses its usual neutral connotation (cf. 1 Cor 11:18; Gal 5:20). Their false testimony is tantamount to "denying the master who bought them." The author leaves undeveloped the redemptive image of Jesus as the one who pays the ransom for our slavery to sin (cf. comments under 1 Peter 1:18-19).

The seductive power of the false teachers seems to be taking its toll. Many will imitate their "licentiousness" a word which in Jude 4 undoubtedly means sexual excess but in 2 Peter may be used more figuratively to include false teaching (note that it is coupled to the following phrase about "the way of truth"). However, this distinction should not be pressed since part of the false teaching seemed to include an irresponsible attitude to sexuality (cf. 2:10,18,19). The intemperance of these false Christians opens the community to ridicule from outsiders. The "Way of Truth" will be reviled because of a lack of integrity in its members. According to Acts the "Way" was a common designation for the Christian community in the early period of the church (cf. Acts 9:2; 19:9,23; 22:4; 24:14,22). The teachers are motivated by greed and they use their rhetoric to exploit people. A number of New Testament texts warn those in authority about the hunger for money (cf. Jude 11,16 and comments under 1 Peter 5:2). 2 Peter will return to this point in 2:14.

2 Peter has no doubt that these teachers will be punished. By denying Christ they bring "upon themselves swift destruction" (2:1). In God's mysterious providence such agonies have been foreseen; "their condemnation has not been idle, and their destruction has not been asleep" (v.3). This long view prepares for the survey of salvation history that follows.

THE RESCUE OF THE RIGHTEOUS AND THE PUNISHMENT OF THE UNGODLY. 2:4-9.

⁴For if God did not spare the angels when they sinned, but cast them into hell and committed them to pits of nether gloom to be kept until the judgment; ⁵if he did not spare the ancient world, but preserved Noah, a herald of righteousness, with seven other persons, when he brought a flood upon the world of the ungodly; ⁶if by turning the cities of Sodom and Gomorrah to ashes he condemned them to extinction and made them an example to those who were to be ungodly; ⁷and if he rescued righteous Lot, greatly distressed by the licentiousness of the wicked ⁸(for by what that righteous man saw and heard as he lived among them, he was vexed in his righteous soul day after day with their lawless deeds), ⁹then the Lord knows how to rescue the godly from trial, and to keep the unrighteous under punishment until the day of judgment.

The author now reviews a bit of biblical history to prove his point about the fate in store for those who pervert the community (cf. 2:3). The entire paragraph is in the form of a long conditional sentence beginning with the "if" in verse 4 and finally concluding with the "then" in verse 9. The conclusion is firmly stated: "The Lord knows how to rescue the godly from trial, and to keep the unrighteous under punishment until the day of judgement" (v.9). 2 Peter borrows heavily from Jude 5-7 in this passage but does not hesitate to alter the material for the sake of his audience.

Three Old Testament examples illustrate the author's thesis. Two of these—the fallen angels and Sodom and Gomorrah—are found in Jude (6-7), but the flood story (2 Peter 2:5) substitutes for Jude's example of the rebellion of the people during the exodus (Jude 5). 2 Peter also broadens the scope of Jude's material: the examples are no longer a rogue's gallery of sinners, now the figures of Noah and Lot become examples of the righteous whom God rescues. The author's line-up of examples also puts these biblical events into proper chronological order in contrast to Jude's jumbled version.

The biblical roots of the angel story are found in Genesis 6:1-4 which speaks vaguely of heavenly beings coming to earth, taking wives and bearing children. Later non-biblical Jewish writings contemporary with the New Testament period such as 1 Enoch filled in the blanks of the story, telling of the angels' fall and subsequent punishment by God. Jude 6 is aware of the details of this legend and counts on his reader's familiarity with them. The sketchy version in 2 Peter 4 suggests that the author has pared down the story because his gentile readers were not aware of these Jewish writings.

The author prefers the flood story (2:5) to Jude's example of the desert rebellion (Jude 4). There are several possible reasons for this choice: 1) The Noah story figured in 1 Peter 3:20 and may have caught our author's eye there; 2) the flood serves as a reminder about the end of the world (cf. comments under 3:5-7) and 3) it would impress his gentile readers who were familiar with epic flood stories common in pagan literature. For 2 Peter the Noah story (cf. Gen 6-9) is an example not only of punishment for sin but of God's rescue of the "just." God saved Noah, whom the author calls a "herald of righteousness" (Noah is spoken of in glowing terms by later Jewish writers such as Wis 10:4 and Josephus) and seven others—a detail of the Genesis story singled out by 1 Peter 3:20 as well.

The Sodom and Gomorrah story (vv.6-8) also takes on positive as well as negative meanings. Jude 7 recalls these perennial biblical badlands as examples of God's punishment for lust and immorality. 2 Peter cites them for being "ungodly," a broader category that includes the errors of the false teachers. Like Noah (v.5) Lot is called "righteous" (v.7). Lot, in fact, comes off much better here than he does in the original story in Genesis 19 and in later Jewish tradition which criticizes him for weakness. However, Wisdom 10:6 calls Lot a "righteous man" and some rabbinic writings concur in this verdict. 2 Peter picks up this positive estimate and makes Lot an example for the Christians. Their faithfulness should make them "vexed" by what they "saw and heard" from the enemies of the community who taught falsehoods and lived promiscuously.

Good people in the community—like Noah and Lot before them—will ultimately be rescued from the "trial" or testing they must now endure. But the false teachers by their distorted lives are already experiencing the harvest of their deeds—a harvest that will be fully reaped on the day of judgement (cf. 2 Pt 3:7).

STRONG WORDS FOR FALSE TEACHERS. 2:10-16.

[10]and especially those who indulge in the lust of defiling passion and despise authority.

Bold and wilful, they are not afraid to revile the glorious ones, [11]whereas angels, though greater in might and power, do not pronounce a reviling judgment upon them before the Lord. [12]But these, like irrational animals, creatures of instinct, born to be caught and killed, reviling in matters of which they are ignorant, will be destroyed in the same destruction with them, [13]suffering wrong for their wrongdoing. They count it pleasure to revel in the daytime. They are blots and blemishes, reveling in their dissipation, carousing with you. [14]They have eyes full of adultery, insatiable for sin. They entice unsteady souls. They have hearts trained in greed. Accursed children! [15]Forsaking the right way they have gone astray; they have followed the way of Balaam, the son of Beor, who loved gain from wrongdoing, [16]but was rebuked for his own transgression; a dumb ass spoke with human voice and restrained the prophet's madness.

These violent words are an escalation of the attack on the false teachers begun in 2:1. The author tosses aside his comparative restraint of the previous verses and now lashes out directly at those he considers poison to the community. Once again he uses ammunition from Jude but freely edits and adapts this earlier letter.

The general principle about punishment of evil developed in his catalogue of Old Testament examples (2:4-9) is applied with special force to those "who indulge in the lust of defiling passion and despise authority" (v.10). Once again 2 Peter indicts the false teachers for their sexual immorality (2:2). The literal wording of the Greek puts it more graphically: "those who walk after flesh with depraved desire." By their teaching and their way of life these wrongheaded Christians also "despise authority." The word used here for "authority" connotes "lordship" and suggests that 2 Peter is not referring to ecclesiastical authority but to the authority of Christ (cf. 2:1, the "master" they deny).

Another trait of the false teachers is their arrogance. This charge is leveled at them in verses 10b to 12. They are not afraid to revile the "glorious ones." In Jude 8 the "glorious ones" refers to the good angels, but in 2 Peter it probably means the fallen angels or demons (cf. 2:4). Though fallen they are still beings of a higher order than humans and hence "glorious." The good angels (v.11) respect this hierarchy of being and do not revile the fallen angels before the Lord. Here is another example where 2 Peter treads lightly around Jewish traditions that may have been familiar to the readers of Jude's letter but were unknown to Peter's gentile audience. The book of Enoch (chapter 9), for example, relates how complaints brought against the fallen angels are relayed to God by the good angels without the good angels offering their own condemnation. Jude 9 gives a specific instance of this angelic restraint in the legend of Michael the Archangel taken from another apocryphal Jewish writing, the *Assumption of Moses*. 2 Peter refers only vaguely to these traditions, enough to press home his point about the blind pride of the false teachers. Their pride makes them like insane rampaging animals (cf. the same metaphor in Jude 10). They pontificate on sacred and awesome things about which they are really "ignorant"—a direct shot that not only challenges the pretensions of the false teachers but reminds the rest of the community about the true "knowledge" given by God and by the apostles' sound teaching (cf. 1:2,3,8,12,16). Once again the author alludes to the final judgement (v. 12); even though the false teachers ridicule the mysterious world of the fallen spirits, they themselves will share in the fate of those doomed angels.

The next barrage (vv. 13-14) concentrates on the false teachers' immorality. Their promiscuity is so bold that they flaunt it "in the daytime," not even having shame enough to seek the cover of darkness (cf. Ecclesiastes 10:16 which criticizes "princes who feast in the morning" and Is 5:11 who scolds morning drinking!). They are "blots and blemishes" (cf. Jude 12) who revel in their "dissipations" and carouse right in the midst of the christian community. The Greek word for dissipation(s) is *apatais* (literally "deceptions" or "enticements"). In Jude 12 the Greek text reads *agapais*, "love feasts." Jude attacks those who are disrupting the christian agape meals with immoral behavior. In some Greek manuscripts of 2 Peter 2:13 the same word *agapais* is found. But the reading *apatais* is preferable. Later scribes may have confused the two similar looking words or tried to bring 2 Peter in line with Jude. The author of 2 Peter probably changed the word from "love feasts" to "dissipations" when he borrowed this section from Jude either because agape meals were not a custom in the churches he writes to or had not, in fact, been abused by the false teachers. But, in any case, their bad example was still in full view of the rest of the community. This lack of respect for the other Christians is noted again at the beginning of verse 14. The false teachers are so engrossed in sensuality that their eyes are "full of adultery"—literally the text says "full of adulterers," that is, they see every woman as an object of lust.

The bad example of the false teachers is not without its effect. They are able to "entice unsteady souls" while they themselves have "hearts well trained in greed" (cf. 2:3). Christians whose faith is not well grounded become easy prey for the smooth hucksterism of these "professionals." This lament will be taken up again in 2:18-19.

Another biblical story (vv. 15-16) rounds out this section. Jude 11 had blistered his opponents for walking in the evil ways of Cain, Balaam and Korah (on the notorious rebels Cain and Korah cf. Gen 4 and Num 16:1-35). 2 Peter singles out Balaam because his credentials as a prophet and wise man fit the false teachers. The author even expands a bit on the Balaam story, not following the biblical account in Numbers 22 (where Balaam comes off rather well) but the later Jewish story which is quite critical of this pretentious foreign prophet. Through some unexplainable error 2 Peter manages to give the wrong name "Bosor" to Balaam's father (the Revised Standard translation politely corrects it to the proper "Beor"). The false teachers have gone the wrong way of Balaam because, like him, they use religious power to exploit people. This affront will be exposed and punished, just as Balaam's attempt to place a curse on God's people was stopped in God's own way—by a talking donkey (this more endearing version of the story is a later Jewish embroidery; Num 22:21-35 had an angel deliver the decisive message).

By their contempt for other Christians and by their terrible distortion and exploitation of religion, the false teachers show their true colors: they are "children of a curse" (v. 14; this is the literal meaning of this Jewish idiom, cf. Dt 11:26-28). The prophetic outrage of the author at this mockery of the gospel knows no bounds.

TURNING BACK FROM THE WAY OF RIGHTEOUSNESS.
2:17-22.

[17]These are waterless springs and mists driven by a storm; for them the nether gloom of darkness has been reserved. [18]For, uttering loud boasts of folly, they entice with licentious passions of the flesh men who have barely

escaped from those who live in error. [19]They promise them freedom, but they themselves are slaves of corruption; for whatever overcomes a man, to that he is enslaved. [20]For if, after they have escaped the defilements of the world through the knowledge of our Lord and Savior Jesus Christ, they are again entangled in them and overpowered, the last state has become worse for them than the first. [21]For it would have been better for them never to have known the way of righteousness than after knowing it to turn back from the holy commandment delivered to them. [22]It has happened to them according to the true proverb, The dog turns back to his own vomit, and the sow is washed only to wallow in the mire.

The concluding portion of the diatribe against false teachers targets the bankruptcy of their enticements. Here the author seems to double back to the opening paragraph of the letter (1:3-4) where he talked about true knowledge, about conversion and about sharing in immortality. These same themes reappear, but now considered from a negative viewpoint since these are the elements of christian life threatened by the false teachers.

Jude's letter continues to be a source for our author's imagery. The opponents are "waterless springs"—a metaphor that improves on Jude's improbable "waterless *clouds*" (Jude 12). The broken promise of a dried-up spring is exactly what 2 Peter wants to say about the false teachers. They are "mists driven by a storm" (another variation on Jude 12)—empty, flimsy, transitory. Their fate is "the nether gloom of darkness" (cf. 2:4). This reference to judgement is an abbreviation of Jude 13 which speaks of "wandering stars" who are doomed to the nether gloom. Jude's more vivid imagery is drawn from 1 Enoch. As he has done repeatedly, 2 Peter avoids references which would presume knowledge of apocryphal Jewish literature on the part of his audience.

The opening salvo about the emptiness of the false teachers and their eventual fate is the lead into the rest of the paragraph. The author gives a stern warning about the enticements of these teachers. It seems clear from this passage (especially vv. 18-19) and others in the letter that their ploy was to claim they were exempt from any moral norms in the name of christian "freedom." Their justification for this brand of freedom may have been the writings of Paul (cf. below, 3:15-17). The apostle Paul himself had trouble with people who twisted the notion of freedom into an excuse for immorality (cf. Gal 5:13; Rom 3:8; 6:15; a similar idea is found in 1 Pt 2:16). Those most vulnerable to this false teaching would be recent converts who had just joined the community and were still trying to find their way. 2 Peter describes them as people who "have barely escaped from those who live in error" (v. 18). Living in ignorance or error was a typical Jewish and christian way of depicting pagan life (cf. above 1 Pt 1:14). The author notes the irony of how those who themselves are "slaves of corruption" (v. 19; cf. a similar expression in Rom 6:16) promise "freedom" to others. A proverbial saying backs up this wry observation: "whatever (or it could be, "whoever") overcomes a man, to that he is enslaved." The false teachers boast of their superior knowledge and dazzle people with their cleverness and daring life-style, but in reality they are immature human beings and hollow Christians because they seek themselves rather than the God who could liberate them.

The situation of the false teachers is truly tragic, not only for the people they lead astray but for themselves—that is the message driven home in verses 20-22. The "they" spoken of in these verses could refer to the new converts duped by the teachers, but the larger context suggests that the author continues to refer to the false teachers themselves. For them to have "escaped the defilement of the world through knowledge of our Lord and Savior Jesus Christ" (a description of conversion very similar in language and meaning to 1:3-4) and then to fall back is a terrible sin. The author quotes a saying of Jesus: "the last state has become worse for them than the first" (cf. Mt 12:45; Lk 11:26). The early church had great difficulty understanding how a Christian once converted would ever deliberately turn away from the gospel and leave the community (cf. Heb 6:4-6). Far better would it be not even to have heard the gospel than, once having accepted it, to deliberately discard it (v.21).

The author calls the christian vocation "the way of righteousness," similar to the term "way of truth" in 2:2. The word "righteousness" or "justice" emphasizes the *action* side of christian commitment (cf. the meaning of the term "justice" under 1 Pt 3:18). To "know" the way of righteousness, therefore, is not simply to be aware of the gospel but to be wholly committed to christian living. "The Holy Commandment" is another code word for the christian life emphasizing action. It does not refer to some specific command of Jesus (as, for example, the love command) but to everything asked of us through our commitment to Jesus. This call for an authentic life is what has been "delivered" or "handed on" to the community by the apostles (v.21; cf. the same thought in 3:2).

To throw this life of love aside and to turn back to a senseless life of indulgence is the awful tragedy 2 Peter struggles with. This regression is its own punishment. Two crude proverbs (v.22) serve to express the author's horror at this sin: the saying about the dog and his vomit is from Proverbs 26:11 and that of the sow wallowing in the mire is found in a number of popular ancient writings (cf. the *Story of Ahikar*). Some commentators suggest that the "washing" of the sow may be a subtle allusion to the baptismal bath that these renegades now spurn. This is not sure. What is certain is the author's complete aversion for what the counterfeit christianity of the false teachers is doing to the community and to themselves.

Part III.

The Day of the Lord.

3:1-18.

The last section of the letter concentrates on the question of the end of the world. Although 2 Peter has completed his major frontal attack on the false teachers (2:1-22), he must still deal with the fallout from their erroneous ideas and bad example. The first part of this section discusses the "delay" of the parousia (3:1-13); the latter part warns against distorted interpretations of Paul's writing (3:14-17). A brief word of encouragement and a final prayer close the letter (3:18).

THE DAY WILL COME.
3:1-13.

3 This is now the second letter that I have written to you, beloved, and in both of them I have aroused your sincere mind by way of reminder; ²that you should remember the predictions of the holy prophets and the commandment of the Lord and Savior through your apostles. ³First of all you must understand this, that scoffers will come in the last days with scoffing, following their own passions ⁴and saying, "Where is the promise of his coming? For ever since the fathers fell asleep, all things have continued as they were from the beginning of creation." ⁵They deliberately ignore this fact, that by the word of God heavens existed long ago, and an earth formed out of water and by means of water, ⁶through

which the world that then existed was deluged with water and perished. [7]But by the same word the heavens and earth that now exist have been stored up for fire, being kept until the day of judgment and destruction of ungodly men.

[8]But do not ignore this one fact, beloved, that with the Lord one day is as a thousand years, and a thousand years as one day. [9]The Lord is not slow about his promise as some count slowness, but is forbearing toward you, not wishing that any should perish, but that all should reach repentance. [10]But the day of the Lord will come like a thief, and then heavens will pass away with a loud noise, and the elements will be dissolved with fire, and the earth and the works that are upon it will be burned up.

[11]Since all these things are thus to be dissolved, what sort of persons ought you to be in lives of holiness and godliness, [12]waiting for and hastening the coming of the day of God, because of which the heavens will be kindled and dissolved, and the elements will melt with fire! [13]But according to his promise we wait for new heavens and a new earth in which righteousness dwells.

The violent rhetoric of the previous section (chapter 2) subsides as the author now concentrates on a major error of the false teachers. They ridicule the whole idea of the Lord's coming, thereby undermining the christian view of history. To counter this false teaching the author reverts to the literary device that has shaped the whole letter—Peter the Apostle *predicts* the threat of the false teachers and rebuts it with sound christian tradition.

The guarantee of the author's orthodox teaching is the first order of business (vv.1-2). The present letter is the "second" one to be written by Peter to his "beloved" Christians. Presumably this is a reference to the First Letter of Peter, and would thus be a rare instance in which one New Testament author explicitly refers to a previous work (cf. also 3:15). Even though the circumstances and style of the two letters are vastly different, they do have some important things in common. Both invoke the authority of Peter and both are concerned with eschatology, the christian vision of the destiny of the world. Both letters, too, exhort the readers to live their lives in harmony with that vision. (On all these points, cf. the General Introduction.) Paradoxically, because the author is actually further in time from the days of Peter the apostle, he elaborates the literary fiction of Petrine authorship more than 1 Peter does (cf. 1:1, 12-15,16-19). So in this paragraph the author recalls that the purpose of his letter is to "arouse your sincere mind by the way of reminder" (cf. also 1:12). What they are to remember is the authoritative teachings represented by the Petrine tradition. These teachings are the "predictions of the holy prophets" whose powerful word is shared by Peter and the apostles (cf. above 1:19 and Jude 17) and "the commandment of the Lord and Savior," a code word for the entirety of sound gospel tradition handed on to the community (cf. 2:21). All of this has come to the Christians "through your apostles."

Some commentators accuse 2 Peter of reducing the vibrancy of the gospel to a series of dogmatic propositions and a concern for ecclesiastical authority. But this is too harsh a judgement and may be influenced by post- reformation disputes. As we have already noted, words such as "knowledge" or "commandment" are not purely intellectual terms for 2 Peter but connote total commitment to authentic christian living. The fact that false teachers threaten to sap the community's life explains the epistle's emphasis on the "truth" and the authority of sound teaching and tradition. It does not mean that the entire christian experience is reducible to these things in 2 Peter's eyes.

The next paragraph (vv.3-4) singles out the key error of the false teachers. These counterfeit Christians ridicule belief in the parousia. In line with the literary form of the letter the apostle Peter "predicts" this as one of the chaotic events of the final days—for the readers of the letter it is now taking place. The author borrows the wording of the pre-diction from Jude 18 where the "scoffers' " wrongdoing is their immorality ("ungodly passions"); for 2 Peter, however, their sin is false teaching. Jewish and christian tradition had always expected troubled times as part of the events leading up to the climax of history (cf. the discussion under 1 Pt 4:17-18). Ironically the very appearance of the false teachers and the disruption their denial of the parousia causes are signs that the end is indeed on its way.

The false teachers ridicule belief in the parousia: "Where is the promise of his coming?" (v.4). The point at issue is not simply the *delay* of the parousia—something that was al-ready integrated into New Testament thought—but the idea that the end would come at all. The false teachers in effect deny that history has any goal; the destiny of the world is an endless gyration of events without purpose or meaning. This is the point of their taunt: "For ever since the fathers fell asleep, all things have continued as they were from the beginning of creation." The "sleep of the fathers" refers to the death of the first generation of Christians. There is little doubt that the early church experienced some nervous-ness as the pioneer Christians died off and the community found itself on the brink of an unknown future. Paul quells the fears of his converts on this very point (cf. 1 Thess 4:13-18; 1 Cor 15) and the climactic text of John 20:29 which blesses those who "have not seen yet believed" may also be concerned with this question. Some New Testament writings had to dampen speculation about the end of the world (cf. Mk 13:12); 2 Peter's problem, on the other hand, is to re-kindle the community's conviction that the world is moving towards its Lord.

The author now unlimbers a series of rebuttals to the viewpoint of the false teachers. The first (vv.5-7) directly counters their statement that creation is unchanging and without purpose. The Greek text of the letter is particularly complicated at this point—a combination of intricate gram-mar, vague style and some baffling variants in the manu-scripts. The Revised Standard translation adequately threads its way through the difficulties and we will follow its lead—even though certainty about the meaning of some words and phrases is impossible.

The author accuses the false teachers of deliberately ignoring the truth (v.5). Creation is not independent of God's salvific work. The heavens and the earth were indeed created by his Word. God formed the earth in the midst of the chaotic waters (Gen 1:2; 6-8). The agency of "water" is stressed by 2 Peter because it leads to his clinching argument. The same God who formed the earth in the midst of the waters to inaugurate salvation history had the sovereign power to destroy that earth through water (v.6). The flood story again serves as a paradigm of judgement (cf. 2:5). The author escalates the effects of the flood—it not only punished the "ungodly" (2:5) but destroyed the entire world. And, he continues (v.7), the same powerful Word of God will move the story of creation to its climax when the world will be destroyed by fire and the "ungodly" will experience "judgement and destruction." So, 2 Peter insists, creation is not a treadmill to oblivion but is tied closely to God's salvific plan.

2 Peter is the only biblical book to speak so emphatically of the destruction of the world by fire (cf. again in 3:10,12). Other biblical authors mention fire as a metaphor for judgement or as one of several torments to be experienced as the world comes to its end (e.g., Mt 13:40-42; Apoc 16:8-9). The reasons for 2 Peter's emphasis should be noted. First of all secular Greek literature speculated on a successive destruction of the world by water and fire. These were not seen as part of an ongoing and purposeful story but as a recurring cycle. 2 Peter may be utilizing this common tradition but transforms it to fit into the biblical story of creation and salvation. Secondly, the author's whole review of salvation history is played out in a negative mode (the flood, Sodom and Gomorrah, fire, etc.) because the errors of the false teachers ("the ungodly") are on his mind. Thus the "judgement" side of God's relationship to his creation is given full play, overshadowing the more positive vision of

creation that plays such a major role in biblical tradition. Only by noting 2 Peter's statements about the flood as the occasion for rescue (2:5) and about the end of the world as the *recreation* of a "new heavens and a new earth" (3:13) is a proper balance restored. These positive statements about a world transformed suggest that 2 Peter's emphasis on "destruction" of the world is rhetorically inflated because he wants to arouse his audience to the threat posed by the false teachers. More important than 2 Peter's use of imagery is his basic conviction that God is at work in our world bringing it to the destiny for which it was created. This is the fundamental tradition ridiculed by the false teachers; for the Christians to lose their sense of purpose would be tragic.

Having directly refuted the false teachers, the author now turns to his "beloved" readers (v.8) in order to drive home his conviction about the destiny of the world. He paraphrases the words of Psalm 90:4 to remind them that God's ways are totally other than our own. The Psalm's equation of a thousand years for one day was used by the rabbis to determine the length of the creation process described in Genesis 1. But 2 Peter's point is not merely chronological nor does he attempt to rationalize the delay by some literary sleight of hand. Rather, the words of the Psalm and the subsequent verses (vv.1-10) are used to emphasize that God's ways are vastly different from our own. Thus the Lord is not "slow about his promise" (another retort to the question of the teachers in verse 4) but he waits patiently out of love for humanity. The theme of God's "forbearance" is strong in the bible, expressed in the recurring phrase he is "slow to anger and abounding in kindness towards us" (cf., for example, Ex 34:6, Num 14:18; Ps 86:15). The identical word used for "forbearance" *(makrothumei)* in 2 Peter 3:9 is found in 1 Peter 3:20 which refers to God's patience towards the generation of Noah. The goal of that loving patience is "not wishing that any should perish but that all should reach repentance" (v.9; cf. a similar thought in

Rom 2:4 "or do you presume upon the riches of his kindness and forbearance and patience [*makrothumeis*]? "Do you not know that God's kindness is meant to lead you to repentance?"; cf. also Rom 9:22). This bold statement about God's will for universal salvation comes as a flash of light in 2 Peter's dark musings about judgement. Similar expressions of God's saving intent are found in both the Old (Ezek 18:22; Wis 11:23) and the New Testament (Rom 11:32; 1 Tim 2:4; Jn 3:16). Affirmed here it not only rebuts the false teaching about a meaningless future but reminds the Christians of their mission in history: the time left before the end should be used to make everyone aware of God's saving love.

Verse 10 reasserts the sureness of the end in traditional imagery. The "day of the Lord" will "come like a thief," a metaphor used in the gospels (cf. Mt 24:43; Lk 12:39), in Paul (1 Thess 5:2) and in the Apocalypse (3:3; 16:15). The author balances out his reflection on the purpose of the delay (vv.8-9) with a reminder that when the end does come it will be according to God's own good time and thus, for us, unexpected and unpredictable. Once again he uses typical apocalyptic imagery to describe the dissolution of the old order. Each "layer" of the universe—the "heavens," the "elements" (the word *stoicheia* probably refers to the stars), the "earth"—will experience destruction. The heavens will pass away "with a loud noise"; the Greek verb *rhoizedon* could connote the crackling sound of the consuming flame. The stars melt from the fire (cf. also v.12) and the earth and "the works that are upon it" (probably referring to all of human culture and civilization) will be "burned up." The final words of this verse have been the subject of considerable debate because of the wide variations in the ancient Greek manuscripts. Among the alternatives to the reading chosen by our translation, the best may be "will be found," instead of "will be burned up." If the verse can be read as a rhetorical question—"the earth and the works that are upon it, will they be found?"—its meaning would not be far from that of the reading "be burned up." The implied answer to the rhetorical question would be that nothing of the old order of creation escaped the fire (cf. Apoc 16:20 where after the great earthquake "no mountains were to be found").

The concluding paragraph (vv.11-13) turns to exhortation, the usual goal of biblical reflection on the endtime. The movement of the world towards its fateful destiny should not lead to fear or paralysis, but to "lives of holiness and godliness." The phrase "what sort of " is not a question but a positive acclamation, equivalently: "What great people you should be, with lives of holiness and godliness!" Unlike the false teachers who ignore the marvelous destiny of human life and creation, the genuine Christians should mold their lives in "expectation of" the Lord's coming. A life of holiness even "hastens" that coming because, as 2 Peter has already noted (v.9), the purpose for the length of time leading up to the parousia is for humanity to work out its salvation. That final day is called "the day of God," an expression for the parousia unique in the scriptures.

The author reaffirms his convictions about the dissolution of creation as we know it, but to the terror of destruction with fire he adds the vision of a new creation (v. 13). Deutero-Isaiah had used creation language to express Israel's longing for salvation. From the chaos of sin and exile, God could fashion a "new heavens and a new earth," a community of life with God where peace and "righteousness" or "justice" would abound (cf. Is 65:17-25; 66:22). Some New Testament traditions draw on that same rich language to describe the christian dream of ultimate salvation (cf. especially Apoc 21:1-5; Rom 8:19-22 may also be inspired by this new creation theology). For 2 Peter this new creation is the content of God's "promise," the "precious and very great" heritage given to the Christians in baptism (cf. 1:3-4). Counting on that promise and working towards its fulfillment are essential parts of the gospel. That is why 2 Peter feels compelled to repudiate the false teachers who espouse a world without meaning.

"DO NOT BE CARRIED AWAY WITH ERROR."
3:14-17.

> [14]Therefore, beloved, since you wait for these, be zealous to be found by him without spot or blemish, and at peace. [15]And count the forbearance of our Lord as salvation. So also our beloved brother Paul wrote to you according to the wisdom given him, [16]speaking of this as he does in all his letters. There are some things in them hard to understand, which the ignorant and unstable twist to their own destruction, as they do the other scriptures. [17]You therefore, beloved, knowing this beforehand, beware lest you be carried away with the error of lawless men and lose your own stability.

The emphatic "therefore" and the direct address "beloved" in verse 14 indicate that the author is beginning to wind up his letter. The first two sentences restate the basic message of the epistle. Since the Christians wait for "these," namely God's promises of a new creation (3:13), they should work at being "found by him without spot or blemish, and at peace" (v.14). This consciousness of a final destiny with the Lord was precisely what the false teachers had attacked (3:4). Their error and their aggressive immorality had earned them the label of "blots and blemishes" (cf. 2:13). The faithful Christians who wait and work for the day of salvation, by contrast, will be found whole and pure by God — just as Jesus himself was designated as the lamb "without spot or blemish" in 1 Peter 1:19 (cf. a similar expression in Jude 24). Theirs, too, will be the great gift of "peace" which Israel and christianity always associated with the final day of salvation.

2 Peter's persistent emphasis on eschatology and his continuing skirmish with the false teachers also mark the opening sentence of verse 15: "and count the forbearance of our Lord as salvation." This repeats the thought of 3:9 which challenged the false teachers who "counted" the delay of the parousia as "slowness" on the Lord's part. History is

not meaningless but is the result of God's loving "forbear-ance," an opportunity for all to experience his salvation. The title "Lord" in verses 9 and 15 probably refers to God rather than Christ, one of the rare instances where this happens in the New Testament.

One more brushfire needs to be extinguished before the author can conclude his letter. Somewhat abruptly a refer-ence to "our beloved brother Paul" breaks into the text (v.15). Although we can only surmise what was going on, it seems that the false teachers were using some of Paul's sayings to bolster their own viewpoint. This is likely to have been on two counts. One would be a misinterpretation of Paul's teaching on eschatology. Later second-century gnostic Christians would use such texts as 1 Corinthians 15:50 ("flesh and blood cannot inherit the Kingdom of God") and Romans 6:1-11 ("so you must also consider yourselves dead to sin and alive to God in Christ Jesus") to develop a purely spiritual notion of resurrection. The human body could not be part of God's redemptive plan and the end had already come in a spiritual way through the religious ex-periences of the gnostic Christians; there was no further "Day of the Lord" to look forward to. The opponents 2 Peter contends with may have taught an earlier version of this kind of error. A second misinterpretation involved Paul's concept of freedom. Even in Paul's own day some members of the community seized on his sayings about freedom and turned them into slogans which justified their promiscuous life-style (cf. 1 Cor 6:12; 10:23; Gal 5:13). 2 Peter had already attacked the false teachers for their immorality and their "lawlessness" (cf. 2:1,2,3,10,13,18) and challenged the counterfeit "freedom" they advocated (2:19). They too, may have been twisting the sayings of Paul to justify their conduct.

So now the author moves to reclaim Paul under the banner of authentic teaching. Once again the device of pseudonymity is invoked. Peter speaks of Paul as a "beloved brother," that is, a fellow apostle. The close bond between

Peter and Paul implied here may actually represent the viewpoint of later history when Peter and Paul were considered the great heroes of the early community. The tensions which characterized the relationship between Peter and Paul have faded under the romantic glow of reverent history (compare Gal 2:11-14). Paul's own writings are given complete respect by 2 Peter. By the time 2 Peter was written the Pauline letters had already circulated widely in the early church and had achieved a quasi-canonical status. Therefore, the author of 2 Peter can state that Paul wrote "according to the wisdom given him (by God)" (v.15)— indicating the divine inspiration of Paul's wisdom and his share in the "prophetic word" enjoyed by Peter and the other apostles (cf. 1:19). The Pauline letters were written "to you," implying not that they were written to the specific communities addressed by 2 Peter, but that the inspired word of Paul belongs to all Christians. His letters are, in fact, counted as "scripture" (the implication of the phrase "the *other* scriptures" in v.16), the only New Testament text so designated within the Bible itself.

The author claims that Paul in all of his letters communicated the same message as 2 Peter does in his (vv.15-16a). It is not clear whether the author has in mind specific passages of Paul. But it is certainly true that the exhortation to live in expectation of the endtime is a fundamental theme of Pauline theology (cf., for example, 1 Thess 5:4-11; 1 Cor 1:7-8; Rom 13:11-14; etc.). On this level Paul's letters and 2 Peter share a basic kinship. Even the summary statement of 2 Peter's message in 3:14 finds strong echoes in Paul: ". . . so that he may establish your hearts unblamable in holiness before our God and Father at the coming of our Lord Jesus Christ with all his saints" (1 Thess 3:13). But, the author continues, there are some things in Paul's letters "hard to understand" (v.16). These were the things pounced on by the "ignorant and unstable." These labels guarantee that 2 Peter is referring to the same false teachers he had blistered in chapters 2 and 3 for their "ignorance" (2:12; 3:5) and the "instability" they caused (2:14). They distort Paul's writings as they do all the scriptures (cf. 1:20-21). But this disservice will lead only "to their own destruction."

The author's purpose is not to discount Paul or to take issue with any of his writings. Some commentators have interpreted 2 Peter in this vein, but there is no evidence that the author himself had any difficulty with Paul's message. In fact he gives the Pauline writings a ringing endorsement (calling them inspired and equivalent to scripture) and offers no more cautions about their interpretation than Paul himself did in writing to his converts (cf. Rom 3:8; 6:1; 1 Cor 6:12; 10:23). Instead, 2 Peter wants to warn the community "beforehand" about the misinterpretation of Paul by the false teachers. The "beforehand" is part of the literary fiction that has operated throughout the letter: in his final "testament" Peter warns of future dangers the readers have already experienced. So warned, the Christians can avoid the "error of lawless men" and not lose what is a precious virtue in troubled times, "stability" (something missing in the opponents and those they entrap; cf. 3:16; 2:14).

FINAL WORD.
3:18.

> [18]But grow in the grace and knowledge of our Lord and Savior Jesus Christ. To him be the glory both now and to the day of eternity. Amen.

The letter had opened with a prayer for the Christians that "grace and peace be multiplied to (them) in the knowledge of God and of Jesus our Lord" (1:2). A similar word of encouragement and a burst of praise conclude the message.

2 Peter entreats his Christians to "grow in the grace and knowledge of our Lord and Savior Jesus Christ." "Knowledge" of Jesus was a favorite term throughout the letter (cf. 1:3). It retains here its usual dynamic comprehensiveness, meaning a total commitment to Christ—a commitment that reverses the "ignorance" of a life without meaning

(cf. 1 Pt 1:14). Unlike 1 Peter the style and tone of 2 Peter has left little room for fervor in its references to Christ. The author's favored title "Lord and Savior" (cf. 1:11; 2:20; 3:2) has a kind of distant elegance typical of his literary style. Yet this style cannot mask the depth of the author's own commitment to his Lord. In most of the letter the author's passion is expressed through his violent opposition to those who distort the gospel and deliberately cripple the lives of weak Christians. But his final word turns from invective to encouragement and prayer: "To him, Christ the Lord and Savior, be the glory both now and to the day of eternity. Amen." This is one of the rare New Testament doxologies directed exclusively to Christ (cf. also 2 Tim 4:18). Even in this burst of praise the author reaffirms that teaching he considers so essential to the gospel: "both now...and to the day of eternity." Christians who shape their lives with that hope-filled expectation have heard the sure Word of God.

FOR FURTHER READING

Beare, F. W., *The First Epistle of Peter*. Oxford: Blackwell, third edition, 1970.

This is a detailed scholarly commentary based on the Greek Text.

Best, E., *1 Peter* (New Century Bible). Greenwood, S.C.: The Attic Press, 1971.

A fine commentary by a first-rate British scholar.

Brown, R., Donfried, K. P., Reumann, J. (eds.), *Peter in the New Testament*. New York: Paulist, Minneapolis: Augsburg, 1973.

This ecumenical study examines all of the Petrine passages in the New Testament, including the two letters, and gives an assessment of the Petrine tradition in the early church.

Elliott, J. H., *The Elect and The Holy* (Supplements to *Novum Testamentum*). Leiden: Brill, 1966.

This scholarly work studies the theology of 1 Peter by a detailed examination of 1 Peter 2:4-10.

Elliott, J. H., *1 Peter: Estrangement and Community* (Herald Biblical Booklets). Chicago: Franciscan Herald Press, 1979.

This brief study is an excellent synthesis of the background and message of the letter for the general reader.

Fornberg, T., *An Early Church in a Pluralistic Society: A Study of 2 Peter* (Coniectanea Biblica: New Testament Series 9). Lund: CKW Gleerup, 1977.

This is one of the few major works on the message of 2 Peter. It is the result of a doctoral dissertation at the University of Uppsala, Sweden. I am indebted to Fornberg for many of the ideas included in my commentary.

Goppelt, L., *Der erste Petrusbrief* (Meyers Kommentar). Göttingen: Vandenhoeck and Ruprecht, 1978.

This excellent commentary is available only in German but it represents one of the finest studies to date on 1 Peter. Many of the late author's insights have influenced my own interpretation of 1 Peter.

Kelley, J. N. D., *The Epistles of Peter and of Jude* (Black's New Testament Commentaries). London: Adam and Charles Black, 1969.

This is one of the premier commentaries on these letters in English. Kelly maintains Petrine authorship in the case of 1 Peter.

Krodel, G. (ed.), *Hebrews, James, 1 and 2 Peter, Jude, Revelation* (Proclamation Commentaries). Philadelphia: Fortress Press, 1977.

Substantial essays on the background and theology of each letter are offered by Gerard Sloyan (1 Peter) and Frederick Danker (2 Peter). Danker contends that the literary form of the "civic decree" (cf. introduction to 2 Peter in the commentary) has influenced 2 Peter.

Selwyn, E. G., *The First Epistle of St. Peter*. London: Macmillan, 1952.

A now classic commentary on the Greek text of 1 Peter.